If You Don't Ask: Close The Sale and Get Paid

ID: 1473335

Category: Business & Economics

Description: How to ask for the order and get paid. After reading this ebook and focusing on closing the sale you will be able to ask for the order in a way that the customer feels good about spending their money with you. You will learn how to guide the sales process towards a predetermined objective that makes it easy for the customer to go forward and make the commitment.

Publisher: Bob Oros

Copyright year: © 2014

Language: English

Country: United States

Keywords: Bob Oros, closing the sale, how-to-close the sale, sales techniques closing, closing sales techniques, closing sales, how-to close sales, closing techniques sales, closing strategies, close the sale,

License: Standard Copyright License

Author: Bob Oros

ISBN: 978-1-304066571-3

ISBN 978-1-304-66571-3
90000

9 781304 665713

Increase your closing ratio

Print these numbers and tape them to your dashboard, they can have a huge impact on your closing ratio...

48% of sales people never follow up with a customer
25% make a second contact and stop
12% only make three contacts and stop
10% make more than three contacts

Here's how you can double or triple your results...
Make at least 12 contacts before you give up.

Here's why:
2% of sales are made on the first contact
3% are made on the second contact
5% are made on the third contact
10% are made on the fourth contact
80% are made on the 5th to 12th contact

"Familiarity breeds contempt," is commonly accepted, but it is not true. In sales repeated exposure leads to a greater appreciation and trust. Exposure and repetition can only increase sales. As a sales person there are several things you can do on a personal level that will make you unique. The first thing you can do is show up - either in person, on the phone, in the mail or in their email inbox.

~~~~~~~~~~~~~~~~~~~~~~~~~~~~~~~

It has been proven many times over that the number of calls you make equals a certain number of sales. The key to this is time management. I found myself with a number of accounts and there was no more time to make call or add more business. Then my manager asked me to layout all my calls on a monthly calendar. As I started to do as he requested I knew he was wrong and this was just a stupid waste of my time. As I got to the last week I found I had time! I have tested this theory many times over with the same results. If you have 100 accounts that you are working, your days are full, no time left to do more. If you lost 25 of those accounts within a short period of time those 75 accounts will fill your days, no time left to do more." In sales numbers are key, but time management is the tool that allows you to do those numbers.

David Vize

Take care of your established customer's needs first and make as many calls as possible the rest of the time. What else is there to do?

Crocker Smith

The more sales calls you make the more closes you are going to have! The more people you get out and see the more closes you going to have. So ask yourself, how much money do I want to make? If your answer is a lot, get off your butt and go make it!

David Bradley

The more sales calls you make, the bigger and better the opportunities become that you run into. I always try to have an objective or a point when I am making my calls, whether it is in person or by phone. I have found that by having 1 question I usually open the door for all kinds of discussion of what is going on internally with that client's company. It grows my relationship with the client as well. I have a few prospects that I know have no "needs" that I can assist them with now, but they may know someone that does…. I still continually check in with these people for our relationship growth. If they ever have a need I am sure they will allow me to help, and they will most defiantly refer me to a friend! Word of mouth can be your best friend or worst nightmare! In summary you can never make enough calls, there are always more prospects to call on!

Brooke Knight

Sales is all about putting ourselves in front of our prospects as much as possible. At times it may seem like we are being "annoying" by visiting them so often. I don't think it's annoying, I think we are showing determination. Even if it isn't a prospective client but a client we already have done business with, we need to be back in front of them because they need to see we care even when there is no order, because we never know when that order will pop up. So how many sales call should we make? More than what we do now, then after that, do more on top of that.

Brandon Sanchez

I am one of the few people who would disagree that more calls can, sometimes, equal more sales. A sales person should focus on what's really important, which I believe is "what to say" when approaching a prospect. Knowing enough information of who your customer is and what their needs are and also knowing enough about your offerings and how that prospect could use your offerings will lead you to better or quality calls, not more calls. You don't want to burn your leads at inappropriate time and then have no people to call. In my opinion it's better to increase the quality rather than call volume.

Yessie Narvaez

I think people get confused when they say the more calls you make the more likely you are to get more sales. Statistically yes, you would get more sales but your ratio would be down. Being from a semi-small town, people here use what they know and who they know. If you can get in and get familiar with business leaders, they will talk.

Matthew Thacker

I believe revisiting the same prospect over and over in a short period of time will produce one of two things; they will either eventually listen to what you have to say or they will tell you to leave them alone and they are not interested in you returning anymore. Either way you will know where you stand.

Lisa Lloyd

I learned the "rule of seven" from my Uncle. He was the branch manager of a brokerage firm. One day, one of the brokers came to his office with a smile on his face saying he had been told "no" for the sixth time from a target client. He now felt the odds were in his favor. We all know it is a numbers game and just have to focus on feeling that familiarity of making numerous sales calls every day.

Gregg Nixon

I agree the more you are in front of a customer the more likely they are going to remember who you are. When you make 1 or 2 calls to a prospect they are more likely to forget due to the number of calls they receive each day from your competitors. If you are the one sales person that is always knocking on their door or calling them then you have a higher ratio of your name/company name sticking out in their mind.

Carla McCrea

Each time you show up, you should have you're A-game on. Because they can become familiar with the bad impression quicker than they will the good impression. Yes repeated exposure is good. It usually takes several calls and visits for someone to remember your company! There is a comfort about going with the familiar product and service. We must make ourselves a name for ourselves, all the while building a strong professional reputation!

Morgan Frazier

I once worked for a company where we were required to make 100 cold calls per day, plus take care of our regular customers and their orders. This is not an easy task but I do realize that the more calls you make the greater your chances of getting new customers.

Vickie Reihl

When to ask for the order

If everything has been done correctly up to the time to close, the close will come naturally. Let's assume we lack just that final touch that puts us in the class of a professional closer. What is that touch? First, the difference between an amateur and a professional closer are that both have the technique at hand; but the amateur uses it so crudely the buyer sees it and resents it. The professional by practice has polished his or her close to the point where it is relaxed and natural. Only one in four (25%) sales people ask for an order after a sales presentation.

Make every call with a specific objective and close on that objective. The amateur, the beginner, still suffers with the delusion that he or she has accomplished something when he just "drops in" for a friendly call. The amateur excuses their lack of closing skill by saying to him or her self, "This will help me get in solid with the buyer." The amateur claims that the call has a lot of advertising value even though they made the call without a specific objective. They do not know that 20% of the sales people take 80% of the orders because they know how to close; that only one in four has a specific call objective and closes on that objective.

To permit the buyer to defer the close is to leave the sale OPEN to a competitor. The Cutting-Edge professional KNOWS that it never pays to leave business on the table. You know that to permit the buyer to defer the close is to leave the sale OPEN to a competitor to walk in and take the harvest when you has planted and worked the crop. The sales person who has polished the technique of closing to professional brilliance knows the fundamental difference between so-called "high pressure" selling and "low pressure". You know the value of intelligent, dramatic, forceful, suggestive closing when you feel in your heart you are rendering a great service by helping the buyer to decide something for the buyer's own good.

You are in the strong position because you have the advantage of working with an organized plan and objective. After all, every sale is a contest, starting with two strikes on the buyer, because you have the advantage of working with an organized plan and an objective toward which you are steering him or her. The buyer is in the weak position of a follower on the defensive. The Cutting-edge professional has learned by sad experience that failure to close, to permit the decision to be deferred lets the prospect get cold, when they might have been sold by the application of a quiet, smooth-running closing technique.

Using the direct close

The direct close is one of the best ways to close because you get it over with up front and there is no doubt about what you are there for. We literally start the presentation with the close. One thing that is extremely important in using this tactic is you have to know exactly what you want before making the call. An example: "I would like to have your ham business, what do I need to do to get it?". "I would like to have your produce business, what would my company and I have to do to get it?"

~~~~~~~~~~~~~~~~~~~~~~~~~~~

Asking for the order and getting the order are two different things. We all want to walk away with an order. You must tell the customer everything about the item you are trying to sell them. Tell them about other customers that are using the product and how they benefited from it. In your presentation you must keep in simple and don't confuse the customer with information they wouldn't understand.

Jim Harris

How to use the choice close

The choice close is the most common close, however, it is often incorrectly used. If we wait until the end of the presentation and then try and squeeze the customer into a corner they will resent it. The correct way to use this tactic is to build it into your presentation by offering two or three different choices, explaining all the differences as well as the features and benefits of each product, and let them choose the one that best fits their needs. For example we could bring three different hams to a customer; a buffet ham, a PIT ham and a football ham. As we were making the presentation we would point out the advantages and disadvantages of each product, letting them make the final decision. The theory behind this close is that we give them a choice between something and something else and let them make the choice. We never want to give them a choice between something and nothing. This close is especially good for the "price buyer". We can show the low quality product, the middle quality product and the high quality product, pointing out that the higher price is really going to cost less in the long run.

~~~~~~~~~~~~~~~~~~~~~~~~~~~~~

We work so hard to get to the close, we have more 'Yes's' than 'No's' but for some reason we fear that closing 'No' - it seems so final that we keep right on selling.

I had a manager call me up and tell me about this new salesman he has hired about eight months ago, "He is a great kid, got the talent, but I just can't get the closing numbers out of him. Could you find some time and work with him and see if you can see what I'm missing to help this young man sell more." Well, I have never seen so many 'prospect's' eyes light up when Jerry stopped by to call on them. As one prospect told me, Jerry is a great guy, has really helped me out.... But he has never asked for an order.

David Vize

Advancing to the choice set up

Nearly everyone in sales knows how to use the choice close; what day would you like delivery, Tuesday or Wednesday? What pack size would be best for you, 12 or 24? You ask the customer to choose between something you want and something else you want and them make the choice - you win both ways.
Now let's take it to a higher level by including the element of contrast. Give them a choice between something they don't want and something they didn't know they wanted until you presented the choice.

Let's say you are going to sell a house to a prospective buyer. The price you want is $100,000. You first take them to a $125,000 house that is overpriced by $25,000. Next you take them to a $75,000 house in need of $50,000 worth of repairs located in a poor area. NOW you take them to your perfectly priced house - $100,000. The choice for the buyer is clear.

How about the used car sales person? They first show you an old clunker that is overpriced and barely runs. Next they show you the care they really want to sell you. In your mind you are comparing the differences and thinking about what a great bargain!

You are talking to a computer sales person about purchasing a new system for your office. You tell the sales person all your requirements who is adding everything up on your list. The sales person now hits you with a whopping $10,000. As soon as you are over your shock you are presented with another choice - a package deal for only $3,000. What a deal! What an easy choice to make. Of course, that is what they wanted to sell you in the first place.

I am at the airport and the flight I am waiting to board is oversold. The attendant jokingly offers to pay $5,000 to anyone who is willing to give up their seat. He immediately admits that he was kidding and says he will pay $200 if anyone would be willing to give up their seat and take a later flight. No takers! Why? He misused the choice close set up. If he would have jokingly offered $25 and then raised it to $200 it would have seemed like a real deal.

Let's say you are going on a job interview and you are going to use the choice close set up. Arrange for two interviews, one immediately following the other. Have a friend go on the first appointment and have them intentionally screw up the interview. Then you go in, well prepared, on the second appointment for your interview and the choice becomes obvious.

If you think this sounds a little shady, consider this choice close set up used by undertakers. The undertaker will first show you a low budget, low price casket that is carefully positioned in a dark corner of the showroom. Then they show you the higher priced casket and point out all the benefits. Compared to the low end casket it is an easy choice to make. The closing statement is usually the one about the how the lower priced casket leaks and the higher priced doesn't! Works for me.

What does this have to do with you? The next time you present a product to a customer take two products instead of one. Take in an expensive, high end product along with the one you want to sell. Show them the over-priced high-end product first. After they get over their shock, bring out the one you wanted to sell in the first place and it will seem like and easy choice.

When I present my sales training program I always make the following comparison:

The American Management Association currently has a program available called Negotiating to Win. It is offered at 13 locations throughout the US at various times during the year. The cost; $1,675 per person with approximately 30% of the information covered being relevant to your business. If you had 25 sales people it would cost you $41,875 plus the individual travel expenses for each sales person. Makes my fee seem low, which it really is!

~~~~~~~~~~~~~~~~~~~~~~~~~~~~~~~

This technique is used on everyone just about everyday. Especially at car dealerships. I remember it being used on me and I left with a car that I would have never purchased. The salesman first showed me an older Honda Accord that needed some work and told me that with my credit that is all I could afford, then all of a sudden the sales manager decides I can purchase the newer model Ford Mustang and bam it was done. Later I realized I hate Mustangs and had been taken for a ride.

Kimberly Burgess

I recently had a sampling with a customer at our location that prepares fresh cut steaks. I knew in advance that the customer was using a lower grade product. I sampled three steaks, one Certified Angus, Choice and his current product. These selections were cuts with a much higher grade than what he was using. We prepared the product right in front of him to sample. He was surprised to find out the difference in taste and texture of the better product. We told him he could improve his menu item for just pennies more to the middle selection. He agreed.

Roland DeGregorio

How to use the guarantee close

Before using the guarantee close you have to be sure your company or the manufacturer will go along with it. It is similar to a closing tactic called the "puppy dog close". The pet store owner tells the parents of the little boy to take the puppy home over the weekend and if they are not happy with it they can bring the dog back on Monday. Of course you know what will happen during the weekend and the dog will never come back. When using this close in a more professional setting you might tell the buyer to try the new coffee machine for thirty days and if they are not happy with it we will pick it up and reinstall the old one. Some companies have even gone so far as to buy out the existing supply of a competitor's product if they agree to try the new product for 30 days.

~~~~~~~~~~~~~~~~~~~~~~~~~~~~

Closing a deal is difficult because a deal is never really closed. When we ask or receive an order that's not the close of a deal that's the end of the sell and the beginning of the relationship. If a deal is truly closed then there will be no more deals which mean no more orders. We want to keep the deal open and continue to service the client and be the go to source for all their needs. If we think a deal is closed because they place an order we are very wrong, that would be the same as if we went to a restaurant placed our order and the waiter or waitress didn't come back, they got the order so why would they need to follow up. Because its never closed.

Brandon Sanchez

Using time as an advantage

The time advantage creates a sense of urgency during the presentation. "While supply lasts" implies that there are several other sales people selling the same program and if you don't put your order in right now you might miss out. "Limited time only" implies that the price will soon go back to the book price. "Sale ends Friday" also creates the feeling of missing out on an opportunity. "One time offer" is designed to put pressure on to take advantage of the promotion now or miss out all together. "Longer shelf life" is also a way of taking advantage of time if the shorter shelf life of a competitor is causing a loss due to waste. "New inventory is higher" implies that the market has gone up and we are holding our price down until we sell out of our current stock.

~~~~~~~~~~~~~~~~~~~~~~~~~~~~~~~

The time advantage close was used to perfection by a local furniture store. First they would have a "Total Inventory Reduction Sale". Then a "Bankruptcy Liquidation Sale". And finally a "Selling Out To The Bare Walls Sale". Of course they never went out of business. They just kept cycling through these sales for several years. But it made you notice them and contemplate going in to see how good of a deal you could get.

Of course, professional sales people know that they would lose credibility if they tried anything like this. But you have to try to give your product some exclusivity along with a slight sense of urgency in the customer's mind to facilitate the close.

Crocker Smith

Trying to close a deal is hard job, giving the customers all information about what you trying to sell them. Getting the customers to talk to you about what you are trying to sell them is very important, they have to understand the whole picture. By the customers asking question will help them make their decision. Asking for the order has to be, after you have given the customer all the facts.

Jim Harris

The trial close to test the buyer

The trial close is designed to lower pressure by using the word "IF". If you decided to buy which portion or pack size would be best? If you decided to buy how many could you sell in a week? If you put this in stock would it benefit your customers? If you stocked this line for one year how much money would it save you?

These trial questions should be part of your presentation. The purpose is to see how close you are to the actual order in a low pressure way. Build test questions into presentation and use them often. The key is to start them with the trial word "IF".

"Ask a question" close

The ask a question close is based on the fact that it is sometimes hard for a customer to say yes, however, it is much easier to for them to say "No". The magic question to ask is this: "Is there any reason why we shouldn't go ahead with this?"

If your first attempt doesn't get the response you want - ask a second time. Wait a short period of time then ask again as if we were asking for the first time. The theory behind this close is the time it takes for a new idea or concept to take hold. It takes time for the mind to work and when we ask the first time there is a natural defense mechanism at work. However, after just a few minutes the buyers mind will start making mental associations and will have more information available to make the decision. Anybody can ask once and accept a negative response.

How to use the last-resort close

The reason this is a "last resort close" is because we should try everything else first. After they refuse to buy, close your presentation, put everything in your brief case and act as if you have stopped trying. In some cases you can actually go to the door, stop, turn around as if you have left and returned as a friend instead of a sales person. This is designed to lower their guard. Then ask the question: "Where did I go wrong?" At this point look at your watch and make a commitment to stay 15 minutes longer. You will be amazed at the difference in the person you are trying to sell.

When to use the silent close

The silent close is the most difficult to use because it seems so unnatural. The hardest thing for a sales person to do is to be quite for 30 or 45 seconds. When there is silence it almost seems like we are not doing our job, however, just the opposite is true. We have to give the buyer a chance to think things over and he can't do it if we are talking away. Keep in mind that the biggest complaint buyers have about sales people is that they talk too much. After the facts have been presented try and remember one thought: Whoever talks first loses.

How prospects make decisions

Have you ever laughed at a joke that wasn't very funny, but everybody else laughed so you felt the obligation to laugh? Have you ever bought something based on the fact that it was the "best selling" or "fastest moving" item? Would the statement "4 out of 5 people surveyed recommend this product" influence your decision? How about "over two million copies sold" on the cover of a book? Would that make you feel more comfortable about your decision to buy it? If so, you are not alone. People are highly influenced and persuaded by what others do.

I am the first customer to go through the car wash, yet the tip jar has 10 one-dollar bills folded in the jar. I am the first one in the bar and notice the bartenders tip jar already has several dollar bills in it. I am the first one to put money in the collection basket at church, yet I notice that there are already several 5 and 10-dollar bills in plain sight.

What does all this mean? It means that this concept works and it can work for you too. Here's how.

Everybody likes to think of himself or herself as a nonconformist – someone who does their own thing. You and I like to see ourselves as independent – until it comes time to make a decision – then we find out what everybody else is doing and what everybody else thinks – and conclude that they must be right – and make the decision that I am going to do the same thing.

Do you see the relevance to your business? Let's say you are a new sales person calling on a potential account. Would you say; 'I am new and don't have any customers yet – will you take a chance and be the first?" If you were a seasoned sales person would you go into a potential customer and say; "We have great quality and excellent service?" No, you wouldn't want to say something like that because their response would be "so what." You would want to take the approach that the bartender, car wash, church, evangelical preacher and concert promoter took. You want to bring on your success stories, testimonials, references, people your prospect knows and a list of happy customers who are buying from you. You would want to put a little money in your tip jar to show that others are buying and they are happy. Why? To make them feel safe about their decision to buy from you.

We find out what everybody else is doing and what everybody else thinks – and conclude that they must be right – and make the decision that I am going to do the same thing. This is the best closing technique of all.

How to close using price

Only 15 percent of buyers change vendors based on a lower price. When your customer understands the value of your offer, price is seldom the real issue. Your customer has a problem to solve and is willing to part with hard-earned money to solve it.

When we are selling a new customer we must sell on something other than price. One of the big mistakes many sales people make is they over exaggerate their claims. They use such overworked phrases such as:

"We are number one..."

"We are the best in the business..."

"You can save big money with us..."

As soon as one of these statements is made a red flag goes up in the buyers mind. We have just "unsold" ourselves. They know immediately that we are not legitimately interested in them. To get them to buy from us we must present a strong case.

The buyers' single concern is their own interest. The buyer has three questions: "So what?", "What's in it for me?", and "Can you prove it?" Facts, figures, and precedents should continually enter into the presentation to justify statements. These facts make the buyer willing to accept you and your offer and make a change based on something other that price. Our goal is to weave the facts into the conversation that makes the customer understand the legitimacy of what we are selling. For example:

"Our program will increase your profits by 6% - here's how."

"This product line will cut your labor cost by 3% - I have the facts right here to prove what I'm saying."

This new marketing system will increase your sales by at least 5% - let me show you what I mean."

A sale is closed when the buyer agrees with our presentation. We are looking for buyer commitment. If you get a customers business based on price - your competitor will take it away from you based on price.

It is always to our advantage to support our sales presentation with backup evidence from impartial sources. Expert testimony is hard to challenge. Having back up information by a third party is a high standard of legitimacy to win their confidence.

What to do after you ask

Beware of the person who agrees to your price too quickly, they may plan on asking for more.

If the buyer agrees to your price too quickly there is usually a request that will be close behind.

"That price sounds pretty good, I will take 100 cases."

"By the way can I have special terms on that?"

Another customer might agree to the price right away and ask for same day or next day delivery. From a buyers perspective this is called the "add on."

Agree to the initial price and then as soon as the sales person starts ringing up their commission, drop the "add on" question. This is also an excellent strategy for you to use as a sales person. Once you have what you want in hand, there is a natural tendency to leave as fast as you can. Perhaps there is an unconscious fear that the customer will change their mind or cancel the order - just the opposite is true.

Once a person makes a decision, their mind works to reinforce the decision. By getting a small commitment first the buyer will start to justify the decision and it becomes easier, not harder, to add on additional items.

Why? Think about your own decision making process. Once you make a decision your mind does a search, similar to a computer doing a search for additional information. Your mind is looking for ways to justify the decision you just made.

Your customer's mind works the same way. This tactic is being used on you every time you buy a car. First the car sales person will get you to agree on color, then options, then an extended warranty, and before you know it you bought the car - one small piece at a time.

The last-minute add on involves throwing in an extra request (usually not so huge as to break the sale but big enough to hurt) at the final moment, just when you, the sales person, has put down your defenses and assumes you have a deal.

The add-on seems to go against a person's nature. "I got what I wanted, I better leave before he or she changes their mind."

To successfully use this tactic, stick around a while. If you are selling multiple items, sell the first one. Wait a few minutes, sell the second one. Wait a few more minutes, sell the third one, and so on. Give the buyers mind a chance to justify their decision.

Remember, they are thinking, "I bought the first one - I might as well buy the second one. I bought the second one - I might as well buy the third one." That is how little orders turn into big orders. It is like going into the grocery store and buying a chicken. I bought the chicken - I better buy the potatoes - the salad - the rolls - the desert - and before you know it your shopping cart if full.

Once you make a decision your mind does a search, similar to a computer doing a search for additional information. Your mind is looking for ways to justify the decision you just made.

Your attitude effects the close

Do you go into each sales call with the HOPE of making a sale, but not necessarily expecting it so you won't be disappointed?

In a recent test researchers found out that if they put a blindfold over someone while they are eating, they eat less. Let's take this another step and ask ourselves this; what if all of a sudden you or I lost our memory and our sight at the same time? What if no one would tell us how old we were and we would have to guess?

What would you say?

Now let's take it another step and ask ourselves what if we were unable to remember any of our past failures and disappointments, but could only remember our successes. What if someone followed us around all week with a movie camera and edited out all the stupid stuff we did? At the end of the week they played everything we did right, every success regardless of how small it was and removed all the bloopers.

Now let's go one step further. Let's say that you are a researcher rather than a sales person. Your job is to do market research and find out why people buy or don't buy. Your success is not going to be determined by whether you make a sale on that particular call, but your success is going to be determined by doing the research.

You make the call expecting people to see you. You expect them to treat you with respect. You expect them to listen to you. You expect them to answer your questions. If the timing is right and what you are offering is the solution to their problem, you expect them to buy. If the timing is not right, or the solution is not a good fit, you would expect them not to buy.

At the end of the day when someone asked you how your day went, how would you answer? Would you say you were a success or a failure? No. You would say I talked to 15 people. Two of them were having problems and I was able to offer a solution. Ten of them were happy with what they were doing but agreed to have me come back at a specific time in the near future. Three of them had very closed minds and were not open to anything new regardless of how bad they needed it.

So instead of making the call as a typical sales person, make the call like a consultant would.

For example: "I am doing some research in the area to find out if our services would be beneficial. Do you mind if I ask you three questions and it will only take three minutes to answer?"

So, if we put a blindfold on you that filtered out the normal fear a person has when approaching a stranger while trying to sell them something, what's left? Confident expectations of doing the job. And the action will create hope, which comes from doing the details of the job exceptionally well. And when you do your job exceptionally well, it is impossible to be disappointed.

Knowing exactly what you want, expecting to get it and visualizing the outcome is effectively managing your confidence level. When you spend time planning your strategies you are creating a situation you desire. You have control over the outcome.

If you are not advancing towards your goal with the expectation of success, it is not the goal that is out of reach. It is the daily activities that need attention. The common denominator of all successful professional people is the same. THEY ALL EXPECT TO SUCCEED.

The common denominator of all unsuccessful sales people is the same. Deep down inside – THEY ALL EXPECT TO FAIL.

Look at a successful surgeon. When they operate on someone they have the positive expectation of success.

A lawyer is another good example. When they are addressing the jury they have the 100% positive expectation of convincing the jury to see things from his or her point of view.

A politician must have the expectation of success. If you interview several candidates running for the same office the night before election, they would all believe they won. If they lost this expectation of winning at any point during the campaign they would immediately be out of the race.

However, there is a difference.

Most professional people must go through several years of higher education before actually starting in their profession. All during these years the attitude of high expectations is slowly building day by day. Once they have invested in four, six or eight years of education they feel they have earned the right to expect success. And they have.

Compare that to the profession of sales. If you have never sold a thing in your life, have very little formal education and are looking for a job – you can start a career in sales tomorrow! The profession will welcome you with open arms no matter what your background, experience or education may or may not be.

In sales you have not had the day-by-day, year-by-year preparation that most professions have. You may go through a short company training program that pumps up your expectations to a high level, however, once you enter the real world, alone and unprepared for what's next, your expectations take a downward turn and things look different.

To succeed there has to be certain things in harmony. Your expectations and your goals must be equal. If your goals are too high or unrealistic you won't expect to reach them and you will see to it that you get what you expect.

Your goals must be clearly defined, realistic, reachable and most importantly APPROACHED WITH THE POSITIVE EXPECTATION OF SUCCESS.

Without the advantage of having four years of sales training before making your first sales call, you have to take a different approach. You have to teach yourself this important principle of selling – to expect success.

Add value to every sale

A sales rep recently told me a great story about how to keep from giving a discount or from having to negotiate the price. He was having the brakes adjusted on his car and the cost was $40. When he asked, "is that the best you can do" here is how he responded: "If you want to negotiate the price – the break job will cost you $50!"

Think about what a great answer that is. What is he really saying? He is saying that I am already giving you the best price I can. He is saying that if you want to negotiate I will raise the price to $50 and we can see if you can get me down to the bottom price of $40.

Try it. If someone asks if that is the best you can offer, quote a higher price and say that is the price for folks who want to negotiate. Or say that is what everyone else is paying and you have already cut the price.

That brings up a good question: Is it part of a customer's job to ask you for a discount? Should you ask for a discount when you buy something? My answer to both questions is absolutely yes! If the sales person didn't ask the mechanic for a discount he would never have learned that great strategy.

I am reluctant with everything I buy and you should be too. The only reason I let go of a dollar bill is to get a better grip on it. I work hard for my money and I want to stretch it as far as I can. So do you and so do your customers. I want to get every ounce of value out of every dollar I spend.

It takes practice to be a reluctant buyer but the dividends are great. By being a reluctant buyer you will learn how to buy everything you buy for less. By being a reluctant seller you will be able to sell everything you sell for more. Just as you play poker to win, not just to make the other players like you.

Your price is based on a lot of factors and making a profit is not optional. You have to get paid. When you study the reactions of people who are trying to sell something to you, a reluctant buyer, you will learn the best strategies as well as see them in action.

It takes GUTS to ask for things and the more you do it the better you are at it. You might be called a few names in the process, but so what.

This reluctance should also be used when you are selling something and asked to lower your price. NEVER GIVE IN TOO EASILY! Never lower your price without setting up several roadblocks, speed bumps and detours.   Let's say I have a car for sale in my driveway with a $1500 sign. You pull in. I immediately go out to the car and take the price down. I have a new sign that says $2500. I explain that I didn't realize the prices were so high and the car dealership would give me so much for my trade-in. I tell you that I will let the car go for $1500 if you try it out and like it and buy it now. But if you come back tomorrow the price will be $2500. You buy it at $1500, the price I wanted to sell it to you for.   You might think that's a little cruel. You can tell that to the person standing next to you in the unemployment line. Or you can get a job at the post office where the price of a stamp is the price you pay! (Sorry, you can probably tell I had to learn all this the hard way).

By lowering your price reluctantly you are actually adding value to your product or service. If you lower your price too easily you will actually CHEAT THE BUYER out of the good feeling they get when they know they got you to come down.

I was sitting on the plane and the woman sitting next to me was in advertising sales. When I asked her what her biggest mistake she ever made in sales, here is what she told me. "I was calling on a pawn shop with my sales manager. He told me the bottom line price for the advertising program was $1,500, but to try to get $2,000 and go down slowly and reluctantly so you "add value" to the program. When the customer asked for the price I made a huge mistake and said $1,500! The customer ended up paying $1,400 and I ended up getting chewed out!"

Here is another reason you should be slightly reluctant when giving a price reduction. An accountant once told me that I should forget the term "gross profit" and replace it with "contribution to overhead." He said that every time I lower the price I am giving part of the company away! The warehouse cost is .04%, the sales department cost is .04%, the transportation department is another .04%, administration cost is .04% and the bottom line should be at least .04%. When you cut your price below .20% think about what part of the company you are cutting out and giving away! Which vacation day would you like to give up? How much do you want you insurance deductible to go up? Which customer service person would they like to tell that they can't buy shoes for their kids this week, etc.

You don't want to appear too hungry for the sale or too eager to give everything away. The buyer will be suspicious and begin to wonder why you are so anxious to make a sale.

When you do have to lower your price never come down in equal increments. If you do you will set up a pattern. The customer will know that to get a discount all they have to do is follow your "pattern" and get a lower price.

If someone asks for a discount, after you've presented your services and quoted a price then you say: "Sure, I can do it for $400, but that would be without the _____ and the _____." You actually eliminate things so that they understand that as the price shrinks so does value.

Another good response when asked to discount your price is to use the "fork in the road" response. Our company came to a "fork in the road" and had to decide if we were going to be simply a price seller or if we were going to be a value seller. We chose to be a value seller and the customers we serve know that in the long run, the value of our high quality products along with our service and support, is like an insurance policy that helps them become successful.

It is necessary to discount your price from time to time. However, you deserve to get paid. Ask your customer if they have any employees who work without being paid. What kind of quality would you expect them to produce? What level of customer service would you expect them to provide to your customers? How much do you think they would end up stealing from you over time?

If your customer's business is down and they are trying to "cut their way into profitability" they are doomed to fail. The only way to increase business and get more customers is by doing it the old fashioned way. By selling!

~~~~~~~~~~~~~~~~~~~~~~

Yes I am reluctant to lower my price for several reasons... Some of which include: I may be leaving profit on the table effecting my bottom line, I don't want to be known as the price guy but rather the guy that brings overall value to the table. After all anyone can slash prices.... Selling an overall value added service that is good for both the customer as well as my company is more what it's about to me.... As well if all I do is slash prices than I will never hit my targets and won't be worth all of the time, money and energy that my company has put into me... In a nut shell just simply dropping my prices doesn't help my, self-worth as a valuable member of our sales team.

Kirel Racovitis

When you exaggerate

I was recently in Toledo and a sales person told me about a friend of his who sells parachutes! He said CUSTOMERS ASK FOR A DISCOUNT!

I always encourage sales people to ask for a discount when buying something to see how the person reacts to your request. However, there are a few exceptions. In certain cases you might want to pay a little extra. For example, open heart surgery. Or perhaps a root canal. And of course it would be a good idea to give an extra tip to the person packing your parachute! In these cases you might even want to take it a step further. You might want to have them give you some PROOF OF THEIR PROMISED RESULTS.

One of the big mistakes sales people and marketers make is exaggerating rather than offering PROOF of the promised results. When you are selling an idea or trying to convince someone of something, you may be tempted to over exaggerate your claims. To get your idea across you may feel you have to use such overworked phrases such as:

"We are number one..."
"We are the best in the business..."
"You can save big money with us..."

As soon as one of these statements is made a red flag goes up in the customer's mind. In your opening statement you have just "unsold" yourself. The buyer, customer or person you are trying to convince knows immediately that you are stretching the truth. The customer always has three questions that have to be answered:

1. "So what?"
2. "What's in it for me?"
3. "Can you prove it?"

Instead of using the above overworked phrases you should use facts, figures, and examples in your presentation or sales letter to justify your statements. These facts make the buyer willing to accept you and your offer. Your goal is to weave the facts into the conversation that makes the buyer understand the LEGITIMACY of what you are saying.

For example, I recently set up a local business with an email system and the results were instant. The company had only 98 email addresses, however, I was able put together a campaign and within 24 hours 52 people opened the email, 25 clicked through, and 10 customers purchased services totaling nearly one thousand dollars. This was business that would have been lost if it were not for the promotion. Needless to say the company is now eagerly collecting the email addresses of their customers.

Like a shrewd attorney, you want to present your facts in the strongest possible light as we did in the above example.

Here are a few more:

"For example our program will increase your profits as much as 6% - here is how."

"For example this product line will cut your labor cost as much as 3% - I have the facts right here to prove what I am saying."

"For example this new marketing system will increase your sales by at least 5% - let me show you what I mean"

An idea is sold not necessarily when you go into your close, but when the customer agrees with your statements - and that is what you are looking for - customer commitment.

The truth is that a customer does not care about you or your program. They are interested in the things that benefit them - nothing else.

It is always to your advantage to support your presentation with backup evidence from impartial sources. Expert testimony is hard to challenge.   Having back up information by a third party is a high standard of legitimacy that will win their confidence.

Precedent is the single most powerful legitimization - precedent is reasoning from a prior sale or situation. Lawyers use precedent judgments to prior similar cases when they make an argument.

What examples can you find in comparable situations that resemble the presentation you are making? The more examples you can find to support your case, the better.

Give examples of actions taken by other customers in similar circumstances. For example: "XYZ Company put the product in and within two month's added $5,000 in additional sales" or "Mary tried this idea in her department and was able to increase output by 23%".

Customers have a natural skepticism about most people trying to sell them something or presenting a new idea. This skepticism is something you should be aware of and prepared to overcome. This skepticism is also a powerful tool YOU can use for undermining the power of the facts or figures someone is presenting to you.

When you are presenting your price and are then presented with a competitor's price that seems much too low, you might use skepticism to your favor. You do this not by debating the accuracy, but rather questioning the source of the price. Without challenging the accuracy or correctness of the customer's position, ask how the price was arrived at.

For example, if the customer quotes a low price - ask where they got the number. Do not object - just inquire as to its rationale. Whenever a statement of fact is made, or a lower price put on the table, or an assumption is put forward as though it were obvious or non-controversial, let YOUR warning bell signal you and ask yourself "Says who?"

~~~~~~~~~~~~~~~~~~~~~~

"When you exaggerate, initially you've blown the whole meeting. As soon as you make an exaggerated comment your potential customer is going to doubt the rest of what you say. They do not care if you are the best or number one, that does absolutely nothing for them. Be legitimate with your statements. Whatever statement you make you should be able to prove it if needed."
Matthew Thacker

"Exaggeration can come back to bite you. If you are being legitimate, you should look the buyer in the eye and do not look away. People read with their eyes and might not think you are sincere if you are not looking straight at them. Ask some of your customers if you might be able to use them as a reference when presenting a product to a new buyer, this should help them see that you are being legitimate about the facts of your product."
Jordan de la Morandiere

"Just today, I called and placed an order for Direct TV. The salesman went through the whole speal and at the end said I need to give him $300 today. I said thank you, but no thank you because I knew he was full of crap. Then he said hold on, let me think, then magically gave it to me for $19.00. I knew before I ever made the call that this is how the call would turn out. Had I of charged the $300, he would have laughed all day at my stupidity. I said that to say this, it's all a game. Sure some people may feel good after having bargained you down to a fair price, but others would not. I didn't feel any better, I just felt like he was insulting my intelligence."

Kimberly Burgess

I definitely like to think of myself as legitimate for sure.... Not that I haven't exaggerated in the past when I was new at selling, however I feel that I have learned from each and every sales call that I've ever done whether it be in this industry or other industries. I love the ability that I have in this industry of many, many years of practical hands on knowledge and experience that I have as a chef/ operator and this is one of the biggest selling features that I bring to the table....When dealing with a customer looking at a variety of products. I can speak from true experience and be a problem solver helping the customer save money in the long run.

Kirel Racovitis

"I am such a penny pincher it would be hard for me to give a discount. I always want to get my monies worth. I am willing to give a "Small" discount to make them feel good about getting us to go down on our price some. I usually can talk them into paying our price because we do deliver what we promise. I know every company has a budget but I have one too. I believe if we have a successful meeting we can come to terms to where I am not losing money and they will think they are getting something for nothing. You have to have your mind set on how far you are willing to drop your price and make sure it is worth it. You must be willing to come to each other terms. They have their mind set just like you have yours. It is like I said they will try to get something for nothing. "

Nina Hall

"Bob, this is one of the lessons from your in person course that I am now using every day. "Is that the best you can do?" I just that daily as a consumer, my husband finds it embarrassing but he likes the fact that many people will actually give you a better deal. On the flip side, when a customer asks me a price, I am no longer lowering my price. I keep it at regular cost and if the customer repeats the cost, I act surprised. I have added several dollars to my bottom line in just the month since I have returned from your training."

Candy Swift

"I have started using this approach more and more with my customers and for the most part it seems to work however you do get those 1 or 2 customers that don't fall for it and say never mind I don't need it. But what I have found out is that the next week that they ask about the same product to see where my price is at, I would usually take it up about .20 and would you believe it they take it. They realize that they better get it now because the price seems to be going up and should have taken up on it the previous week. Live and learn and I say."

Sarah Jones

"Very good information. I'm in the process of looking for a car right now and I think this will come in very handy for me. I need a car so badly that I was willing to just take what I could get, but now I feel armed with a good bit of valuable information. I will try this tactic when I sit down at the table with the sales person. I'll let you know how it goes."

Brian Spraggins

"Being reluctant to give a discount makes the buyer feel like he has won the battle after the sale has been made. Also, if the buyer is happy then he will most likely turn into a repeat customer. When someone asks for a discount and a number pops in your head to take off the original proposal, split that figure in half or even thirds and see where it leads. Example: Seeing certain figures on paper or anywhere for that matter is all a head game. Which looks better…$4,000.00 or $3,900.00? Just by reducing the price by $100.00 can make it look much more appealing to a buyer. "

David Bradley

"A day late and a dollar short! I needed this lesson two weeks ago. I am normally fairly good with negotiations; this one client wanted to go straight to the bottom line, which I did. NOTE TO SELF: Don't give out your bottom line number!!!! I gave him the bottom line number and 2 days later he came back with a lower price. They were adamant on not paying what we bottom lined. Moral of the story- I lost $$$. Ouch- expensive lesson. Been there, done that and it won't happen again."

Teresa Cloninger

"Automatically reducing your fee is making a statement that you are not confident in your own ability to deliver a good/better product or service to the potential customer. I feel it says that a person does not value their own self worth. I'm a firm believer if I going to work hard to deliver an excellent service that I should be compensated for my effort and diligence in providing that service. On numerous occasions I have encountered sales people that just give it away without a fight, resulting in loosing money not only for the company, but themselves. The number #1 reasoning I hear is "we have to lower our prices because our competitors are" My thinking is if the customer is taking the time to discuss their needs with you, then the competitors they are currently working with at a lower rate must not be doing something right, otherwise the customer wouldn't be talking with other vendors. Sale people should not focus on "all" the reasons why they need to reduce their fee, but concentrate on all the reasons why they "shouldn't" reduce their fee.

Carla McCrea

If you are going to talk to customers about products I believe you should always have information to back it up. I always like to have a fact sheet on the items that you are talking about. I know we all like to Exaggerate a little to make it look bigger than it really is. Don't do it with customer….. because it well catch up to you.

Just tell it, the way it is, I believe the customer well respect you more. Always know the information before you see the customer so you don't Exaggerate and look like a fool. Remember you want to build a good rapport with the customer, so you have to know the facts. Don't Exaggerate you have to be honest they will see right through you. Make sure you can back up what you are telling them.

Jim Harris

Responding to price shock

Not long ago I attended a two day seminar designed for buyers. The seminar was about teaching these professional purchasing managers how to be better negotiators. The instructor started off with an example about how a company implemented just ONE negotiating strategy for one year to see what effect it would have on the company's profit. After the year was over the company was able to show an improvement of one million dollars strictly from this one concept.

They had a more glamorous name for this powerful strategy, I simply call it price shock! And it is one of my best techniques to use as well as to talk about.

The best story I have ever heard about price shock is from a buyer who claimed he could get a sales person to lower their price without saying a word. He said he was able to perfect his "price shock" strategy by practicing on his way to work every morning.

What exactly is "price shock?" It is a simple facial expression that says, "Your price seems high!" Well-trained buyers are taught to use this strategy with exact precision.

When a buyer is looking at your initial price they are taught to wrinkle their forehead as if to say "you are much higher than I expected!" This is designed to immediately put you, the presenter, on the defensive. The sad part is, it works most of the time. Even if you have a close relationship with the buyer, you may misread it as a sign that you should lower your price to get, or keep, the business.

Work on your own price shock until you can perfect it. Every time you buy something act surprised at the price. Watch closely how the seller reacts. If you are buying a new house, tell the realtor you are shocked by the price. When you are in the market for a new car, try it on the car sales person. When you buy a new TV, tell the clerk you are shocked at how much the price is.

To become an expert at how effective price shock is you should practice your own unique style for acting surprised every time a price in presented to you. Whenever you are given a price on anything, act slightly surprised – watch carefully how they respond. Simply say "the price is a little high", or "I am sure this is a nice hotel, however, your price seems a little high", or "I was thinking about buying a new boat, however, your price seems a little high!"

For example, a large horse trailer dealership in Dallas was setting up a meeting for all their sales and management people and needed to book a large block of hotel rooms. This was right after they attended my seminar and they decided to give it a try. He called me and said the results were amazing. The savings was $2500. Not bad for a little theatrics.

Do I use this strategy – absolutely – I use it every time I am presented with a price! I stay in many hotels during the course of a year. Does price shock save me money? One hundred hotel rooms x $10 average savings = $1,000 per year!

When I check in I ask for the price – act slightly shocked – pull out my deck of discount cards – act shocked at the discount price and many times get a lower price than the lowest discount.

What about when someone is shocked at YOUR PRICE? What should your reaction be? There are four responses you can use to counter this powerful strategy:

1. You can be weak, give in, and lower your price. They won. This is what most buyers expect, especially from an amateur sales person.

2. You can be shocked at their shock. This is designed to neutralize the strategy. The customer is shocked at your price; you are shocked at their shock. Seems a little strange to use at first, until you see how well it works. This throws the shock right back at the buyer and you have now put the buyer on the defensive. Then stay silent. Do not provide an explanation. It is the buyer's turn to make the next move! This is so effective you will have a hard time keeping a straight face. Role play this and get it down to a science.

3. You can use the "Feel, Felt, Found" reply. Here is how it works: "I understand why you feel that way, everyone I talked to so far today felt the same way, until they found out that the market has gone up since last week."

4. You can justify your price rather that discount it. This is an extension of number three. "I understand why you might feel that way, everyone I talked to today felt the same way, until they found out what is included in that price." And then begin to list the additional benefits that are included, which makes the price seem smaller and smaller.

5. There is a response called a "fork in the road" response that sometimes works on price shock:

"Our company came to a fork in the road and had to make a choice on whether to be a low cost, no service, no frills type of company, or to be one that provides services, follow up, and extra benefits. We chose the latter. One other thing to consider Mr. Prospect, you get me. I go with the deal - and if you don't think I can make a difference - try me."

Bottom line - There are plenty of folks who want to buy just on price and the sales people who sell them could be replaced with a fax machine.

~~~~~~~~~~~~~~~~~~~~~~

"Whenever possible, don't discuss price until you've discussed the validity of your pricing. If forced to give a price prematurely, only offer a range. Ask questions that will help you understand what the client wants. Always add 10 to 20 percent to your high end. It's a lot easier to go back with a lower price than a higher one. If the customer is going to choke on your artificially high price, he'll choke on your real top end price, and you'll lose the advantage of being able to quote a final price that is lower than he expected.

Yessie Narvaez

"I try to avoid the "Shock" effect altogether. I believe in managing expectations up front. 1st I find out if they have used a similar service in the past; if not I walk them through the process and briefly mention the cost (giving a wide range). This should prepare the person for negotiations. If they try to use the "Shock" effect – don't flinch. Counter with the "Triangular negotiation" method. Here you are negotiating three different variables; if you change one side- I change another side. So no matter what type of triangle you end up with (right, acute, obtuse, equilateral, isosceles or scalene) its still a TRIANGLE. A win-win-win for every one."

Teresa Cloninger

"I never thought of reacting to shock with shock---I always thought I had to explain why or "attempt to get a lower price". It works though...I tried it by simply saying "REALLY!!" with a bit of shock on my face and said nothing else....He bought the product and we moved on like nothing happened."

Ken Jones

"I actually used the shocked approach yesterday when it was tried on me - IT WORKED! I said that the previous person had the same shock when they saw the price of the meat slicer, but when I explained that I came along with the deal for service, and explained how the unit would assist with profitability, and that I helped them save a lot by directing them to the unit they need to fit their needs... they found that the price was great, and purchased immediately. We got to the 'fork in the road' moment, where I thought I might lose the sale, and went silent. They were a little thrown off, and about ten long seconds later, they asked for the slicer to be boxed up, and asked if I could assist them in finding the rest of the wish list they were carrying. That was a big sale, and an especially happy customer."

Craig Young

"Price shock immediately gives you a sense of guilt, which you have to learn to overcome right away and be ready with a come back. A lot of buyers are shocked at the price because they do not understand the quality of the product such as a home use item compared to a commercial item. Our job is to convince the buyer that it is the right product for their needs, and a good value for their money."

Jordan de la Morandiere

Yes, I believe most customers are always shocked about the price. It does matter what the products are. Everybody wants a cheaper price even, we do when we are shopping for our self. You have to stand your ground on the price you give the customer. But before you give a customer a price you have to know the facts,

What is there volume, how many delivery's to they need, what kind payment terms to they want. With knowing the facts about the customer, this will let you set the price, so when you tell them they wouldn't be shocked. Don't back down from the price, because if you do. Every time you do give them a price on a new product they will try to beat you up for a cheaper price.

Jim Harris

The higher authority strategy

A good lesson learned a while back was from a sales person in Twin Falls, Idaho. A friend of his sold a service station to someone from another country that didn't understand how we do business. The new owner would order a part from the auto supply store and then try to negotiate the price with the driver.

You may be thinking how anyone could do something that dumb. However, if we go into a customer's business and are not talking to the decision maker, we are doing the same thing.

Another perfect example of this strategy in action was demonstrated while checking into a hotel in North Platte, Nebraska. I asked the clerk at the front desk for a discount. She said she had to check with the manager and went back into the office. When she returned she said she was sorry but the manager said that was the best they could do. I walked over to the elevator and while waiting another person came in and asked for a discount. The clerk did the same thing only this time I could see the entire office. It was empty. She simply walked into the office, stood there for about five seconds and returned.

Sometimes a decision maker will use a "higher authority" to hide the fact that they are the decision maker. For example: "This agreement looks good, but I will have to run it by my committee (or wife or any other higher authority)."

Using the higher authority is when the customer or prospect does not have responsibility for making the buying decision. It is usually a "buying committee" that has the final say.

The next time you buy a house or car watch carefully how the sales person will remove this roadblock. The sales person will say, "If we find the house (or car) that you really like, is there any reason you could not make the purchase today?" Once they get the green light, the sales person will spend whatever time it takes to find you the right product. If you say your husband or wife has to give the final approval, the sales person will try and set up an appointment when both of you can be present.

To avoid being the victim of the higher authority, be sure all parties necessary to make an agreement when you are making your presentation. For example, if one of the buyers is not present, it is best to postpone the meeting until everyone can be there. If one of the critical parties is not there, that person can veto everything that was agreed upon.

If you are the one making the presentation and the presence of someone important is impossible, set a short one or two day time limit for his or her higher authority approval.

You can use this same strategy. You can start your presentation with the same question. "If I show you a program that will not only save you money on your operating expenses, but also lower your labor cost as well as increase your sales, is there any reason why you would not want to give it the go-ahead?" If the buyer has to get approval from a higher authority you will know how to tailor your presentation.

If you are making a presentation to a person who does not have authority to make the decision, the best strategy is to build up the person you are presenting. Suggest to the person that the committee is surely influenced by what he or she says. If you can get them to commit to making a "sale" to the committee, it can be embarrassing if he or she is not able to get it through for you.

Another strategy if you are selling to a buyer who has to "run it by the committee" is to ask about the possibility of making a presentation to the committee yourself. This can either call their bluff or it may present you with an opportunity to actually make a presentation to the buying committee.

When making YOUR presentation it is to your advantage to present a higher authority from which you must get approval. Even if you do have complete authority over the selling price, you may want the buyer to believe you have to get approval.

If both buyer and seller could say to the other, 'I know what I am doing and I have the power to make the best deal possible' it seems as though the selling process would be much easier. This is not always the case. When you have the authority to make the final decision the buyer knows that he or she only has to convince you and does not have to work quite as hard if you are the final authority. Once you have given your okay, the sale is done.

Not so with the person who has to answer to a higher authority. When you have to have approval from your department manager, sales manager, purchasing manager, marketing manager, or even the president of the company, then the customer must do much more than convince you, he or she must present a reason you can take to your higher authority for approval.

This is only a tool you should be aware of and use when the situation calls for it. There are many times that it is not necessary and you can be the final authority without any problem.

"Every salesperson should know how important it is to have the key players in the room before you pitch your product or service. The logic behind this is that whoever you pitch to is going to go to the decision maker and try explaining what you told them and who knows what there going to say or how they are going to make your product or service look. Nobody should know your product or service better that yourself, so don't you think you need to be the one selling it and not some schmo sent there just to make you think your doing your job!"

"A good question I learned a long time ago is "Other than "_____", is there any other reason we can't do business today. If its Price, Other than the price, is there any other reason we can't do business today? This is a great question to ask to find out exactly what you need to fix or change, to make the sale today!"

David Bradley

Unfortunately for high dollar services there is a Higher Authority or Two or Three…… The best case scenario to ask about making your presentation to everyone at once. I don't seem to live in that magical little world. Sometimes you have to overcome the objections one at a time- one level at a time. One thing I have found helpful as you get buy in at each level; ask what objections you think the next level will have. This helps you be a little more prepared and the more buy in you have the better. Hey, if life was easy- what fun would it be?

Teresa Cloninger

I think this is a very interesting concept. I have often used this, without having truly thought about it and the process. One thing I do realize from this lesson is that, by offering to make your presentation to the committee or decision maker, it takes some of the pressure off of the non-decision maker. I have seen relief in a front office person's face, when I asked to speak directly with the decision maker. Not only have you gotten to the person you really need to speak to, you have also forged a more comfortable relationship with the person who can get you there.

Tonya Sauer

There are many uses of the higher authority strategy and you should understand how it works so that you can respond effectively when they are used against you. One of the most common uses is to obtain a delay without directly asking for one. In this way, the absent authority provides an opportunity for the salesperson to go back, think through the positions of each side, and evaluate the proposed agreement. It works for me!

Yessie Narvaez

I knew a guy that owned a communications company and had vice president as his title on his business card. Even though he owned the company, he always had an "out" to use the higher authority whether he was selling his product or someone was making a presentation to him. It is definitely a good idea to build up the person who is not the decision maker. Making them feel they are part of the process for a major decision is great way to get them on your side.

Gregg Nixon

Many times I might say to an individual "I know you don't want to hear all of this twice. Is there anyone else who will need to hear my information today?" You would be surprised how many times the prospect will say " Let me see if Joe is busy" or "Maybe Sherrie can meet with us, too. I also might say "This is a lot to remember. Would you like anyone else present so you don't have to ………

Lynn Mosely

Good guy – bad guy strategy

Good guy/bad guy is taking the higher authority strategy to the next level. The good guy/bad guy can be obvious or it can be quite subtle. It can be carefully planned in advance, or people can fall into the roles naturally.

When this buying strategy is used, you might not even notice until you have become the victim. The real estate agent and client often use this method. For example, the home seller might play the bad guy, holding out for top dollar. But the seller's agent plays the good guy by showing the bad guy why the price is above market value.

Husband and wife teams often use this method too. The husband is usually the bad guy while the wife is more reasonable and sympathetic to the other side's viewpoint.

Good guy/bad guy occurs when there are two or more buyers and one is easier to get along with, provides more information, or seems more anxious to make a deal, while the other is more difficult.

I recently sold a travel trailer and was amazed at how most husbands and wives fall into these roles. The wife would make the initial call and get all the information before handing the phone over to the husband, the bad guy, to talk about the price.

We have all seen the good guy/bad guy tactics on television. A suspect is caught and interrogated. The first detective puts him under a glaring light, hits him with hard questions and roughs him up.

The tough guy leaves. In comes the nice guy who gives the suspect a cigarette and lets him relax. Soon the suspect spills all he knows.

Car dealerships are known for this. When the sales person says "I will take this to the sales manager and see if I can get this price for you", they actually make us believe they are on our side!

Here is how it works in a car dealership. Let us assume you and the salesperson have reached a price agreement. The salesperson has to get "approval" from the manager "Bad Guy" to honor his/her agreement with you. However, only the sales manager can accept an offer. The salesperson is a messenger between you and the sales manager.

The next time this is strategy is used on you - try this: tell the sales person that you want to go into the sales managers office together - you want to see how the sales person is going to work for you to get the price you want. They will tell you that is not possible - insist on it.

You can do the same thing when a buyer insists on a lower price. You can call your manager (the bad guy) and report back that the manager was really tough on you, "However, I was able to get the price down a small amount. Not quite what you want, but pretty close." This makes the customer believe you are on their side.

When faced with the "good guy/bad guy" routine do not fall for it! The buyers both have the same goal - to get you to give everything you have.

Another heavy-handed but effective tactic of intimidation is to out-number the other party. You show up alone; the buyer brings in the lawyer, the accountant, the executive vice-president, and so on.

If you think your opponent is using Good Guy/Bad Guy, do one of two things. Let the other side know you have recognized the tactic, or bring in a Bad Guy of your own.

Good Guy/ Bad Guy is a very effective way of putting pressure on people, without confrontation. Counter it by identifying it, people use this tactic on you much more than you might believe. Don't be concerned that the other side knows what you are doing. In fact, when you are negotiating with someone that understands all of the gambits, it becomes more fun!

Yessie Narvaez

Actually, depending on the good guy/bad guy routine, you can work it to your advantage. For example, I bought a brand new car 2 years ago. I took my brother in law in with me to use his discount (since he's an employee of that car manufacturer). The sales person used the whole bad guy/good guy routine. Payments worked out to 5 years at X dollars per month - but only came with a selected warranty. That was the best price he could give me.

The next day, I go in, sign the papers, and then I'm waiting for the sales person to bring my new purchase around. I was walking around the dealership - and right into the sales manager's office by mistake. I talked to him for a few minutes and told him that I was surprised myself that I bought another car from that manufacturer, considering I had been lied to by the sales person when I bought the car prior to that one (same manufacturer). I went out, and grabbed stuff from my old car.

Before I left the dealership, the sales person called me in - the sales manager came up with a new deal. Payments were then a little lower than X dollars per month, for 4 years, and with a bigger warranty package! The point is to recognize it, and work it to your advantage!

JoAnne Welch

I hate playing games- I don't like the Good Guy / Bad Guy routine. There is nothing wrong with negotiations; but the bottom line is the bottom line. Sometimes it is better to walk away from business. Not all sales are good. YES you heard me right- sometimes it better to turn down the business. If the customer is playing games now- what will they do in the future? Can they be trusted? Ask a few probing questions and see if the buyer really has to get approval from the "higher authority". IF not and they are just playing games; ask them to give you a call when they grow up. Just say it nicely!!!! Truth in Sales,

Teresa Cloninger

Most car repair shops think that when a woman comes in she dose not know anything about cars. Well, I have replaced many things on a car or truck from a fan belt, water pumps, engine gaskets, and all the way down to the UV joints. I don't claim to be a pro but I do now how to do these things and understand some car repairs are harder than others. I usually get my own parts and then call the different shops to see who has the best price on installation. Some still try to quote me prices that are too high in my opinion, and if they do I bring in my husband to play the part of the bad guy.

Laura Arnett

Is that the best you can do

This seven-word strategy has the power to save you thousands of dollars each year. If you use this seven-word question seven times you will save money. I use this strategy every chance I get.

Here is an example. I had a meeting in San Jose, California and when I called to reserve a room the price was $289 for one night.

My reply was $289 FOR ONE NIGHT? I live in Oklahoma, that's a month's rent, including utilities! The lowest I could get them down to was $269.

Instead of taking the room I decided to drive around looking for something a little less expensive. I came across a name brand hotel and asked the clerk how much a room was for the night. The woman behind the counter said $189. I decided to use the "is that the best you can do" question - also called "the squeeze" - and see if I could get a discount.

My first tactic was to use price shock. She came down to $169. Next I asked her if that was the best she could do. She came down to $149. Then I asked her if she had any specials going on and she lowered the price to $99. I asked her one more time if she could do any better explaining that I was on a tight budget and anything over $100 (including taxes) would cause me a lot of problems.

She lowered the price to $89!

TWO HUNDRED DOLLARS less than what the first price I was given when I first came to town! There are several things she could have done to get a higher price.

First, she came down too easy and too fast. If she had been slightly reluctant I would have stopped asking for a lower price.

Second, she could have said it was obvious that you have not checked the price at the Hilton - I would have stopped asking for the lower price.

Third, she could have said she had to check with the manager (higher authority) and walked in the back room for a moment - returning, she could have said the manager would not let her go any lower (even if the manager was not in the office).

Fourth, when I was shocked at her price, she could have acted surprised at my shock. This would have stopped me by making me feel slightly embarrassed - well, maybe a normal person would have been embarrassed.

This seven-word statement has saved me an untold amount of money over the years.

I was recently in Los Angeles working with a group of sales people and the "is that the best you can do strategy" was thoroughly explained. One of the sales people called me the next day and said he was able to save TWO THOUSAND DOLLARS on a software program he was buying.

I was working with a group of sales people in Las Vegas and a sales person called me the next day and said he was able to save EIGHT HUNDRED DOLLARS on a landscape project he was purchasing for his new home.

I was in Allentown Pennsylvania and one of the managers called me the next day and said he was able to save FIVE THOUSAND DOLLARS on a contract he was working on.

What should you do when someone asks you if that is the best you can do?

First, simply say yes.

Second, if they insist on a lower price you can consult with your "higher authority."

Third, if they still insist you can turn your higher authority into a "bad guy".

Fourth, if they still insist on a better price and you feel that to give in a little will guarantee the sale, you might come down on your price a very small amount and act as if you are really going out on a limb and taking a chance (reluctance).

~~~~~~~~~~~~~~~~~~~~

I really enjoyed the training in Richmond. I used "is that the best you can do" on the airline after I missed my connection flight back to Sarasota. I was given a free hotel, dinner, breakfast and $100.00 off my next flight. So yes it does really work.

Timothy Emmett

I am going to do a little experiment this weekend. At EVERY garage sale I attend, I will ask "Is that the best you can do?" - even if it is on something that costs $.50. I can't wait to see how much money I can save on items that I'd usually pay the sticker price for! Morgan, my co-worker is coming with me, so I will have a witness to be sure that I follow through with my plan. Once I see it in action, I will definitely be compelled to use this when making bigger purchases. When someone poses this question to me, surprisingly, the word "Yes" does wonders. People have the same thought that I do..."At least I asked."

Laura J. Czajka

I have used all four tactics, depending on the situation. The reluctance tactic is most popular. I tried (is that the best you can do) the other day. I do know if I was getting a great deal, but I asked anyway. The salesperson (owner) simply said yes, and I could not get them to go lower.I did feel a little guilty, but not as much would have been in the past - so I am making progress.

Jordan de la Morandiere

I love this concept. After reading this I gave it a try. I made a reservation at a hotel. They told me the cost would be 119.00 for a king room. I ask, "Is that the best you can do?" He then told me he could give me a two doubles for 109.00. I replied, I have stayed at your hotel in the past and will more than likely stay again, but not at those prices. Long story short, I paid 75.00, for the king. I am so excited that this worked so easily I can't wait to use it again.

Tonya Sauer

I like this response because I think we forget to ask this of our vendors that we work with on a daily basis in our offices. To our equipment company, 'is that the best you can do?', to our office supply company, 'is that the best you can do?', to our t-shirt supply person, 'is that the best you can do?' We must be prepared to respond to our clients as well when they ask the same of us. All of things our cost covers should be in our response to this question. 'Why yes, Mr. Customer, that is the best we can do based on the following: Fica, Futa, Suta, Workers Comp, administrative fees, recruiting fees, qualifying fees, background and drug testing...etc.'. We too are in this business to make money, so yes that is the best we can do.

Kristan Wilson

Overcome every objection

Abraham Lincoln had a reputation as a lawyer for hardly ever losing a case. His strategy was to unknowingly use the feel/felt/found formula to perfection, however, he probably never heard of it.

Lincoln would never argue or attack an opponent. In fact, Lincoln, at first, would argue his opponent's case telling all the reasons why his opponent was right. He'd appear to agree to all the things his opponent said.

As his opponent was stating his case before the jury Lincoln would write down everything that was said. Then he would begin changing the minds of the jurors by saying, "We all feel these things are true, and my opponent has skillfully presented them in a way that anyone hearing them would have felt the same, however, there are a few other things that influence this case and when I present them you will find that the way to vote will be obvious."

Then he'd begin slowly with his own arguments. He was a master at diplomacy, at getting people to change their minds and feel good doing it.

Lincoln probably invented the "feel/felt/found formula even though he never heard of it. The feel/felt/found formula can become one of your most valuable tools. Try this response when you get a negative reaction to the price you are presenting or the program you are trying to push through.

"I can certainly understand why you feel the price seems a little high".

"I don't blame you for wanting to get the best value for your money and at the same time keeping your cost down to a minimum."

"Every person I talk to has felt the same as you do when they first looked at the program".

However, after they found out that the small difference in price for the higher quality product was actually the best investment they ever made they saw it from a completely different view."

Practice this a few times and people will never know why they are all of sudden agreeing with you.

I understand how you FEEL…

Everyone I talked to today FELT the same…

Until they FOUND out that the market has gone up!

~~~~~~~~~~~~~~~~~~~~~~~

I can see where this tactic could be beneficial in some situations but not every. It all depends on the client you are pitching too. Also, the product or service that you're selling is a factor. Once you get to the point where you say, "know why you feel this way", you have already gotten them worked up or mad or put on the defensive side. Then if you come back with, "everybody else felt the same way," well they are going to wonder why the heck you still trying to sell something that gets everybody all worked up. Maybe you should see a pattern of previous clients getting defensive about what you are selling and try something new. Basically, I am saying make it sound irresistible and pitch it right the first time, close the deal and move on to the next potential client!

David Bradley

Nothing takes the wind out of someone's sails faster than when you use this strategy! When you start with an agreement it befuddles them. I remember once during a debate in college when I used this approach- my opponent spattered and sputtered "you can't agree!!!" I continued on using facts that turned that agreement around. I won. Our minds are always racing- the buyer is already coming up with the next answer to what they THINK your objection to their objection is going to be. (You know when they get that smug look on their face.) Sometimes you have to short circuit the opponent's brain to get them to stop and listen to you. This is one approach that definitely works.

Teresa Cloninger

The great thing about this tactic is that gives you extra time to change people's mind when necessary. Sometimes, something will come up in a negotiation that you were not expecting. You have not heard anything like this before. It shocks you. You do not know what to say; but if you have Feel, Felt, Found in the back of your mind, you can say, I understand exactly how you feel about that. Many other people have felt exactly the same way. However, by the time you get there you will have recovered your composure and will know exactly what to say.

Yessie Narvaez

This is a grand strategy. It also explains a lot about this dynamic individual. Having the ability to turn the tables on your client without them realizing it would be a great skill to develop and the neatest part about the plan is that you are not being dishonest with them in any way, you are simply starting from the side they are most likely already on and allowing them to convert to your beliefs on their own terms. This is a lesson I would like to learn and implement.

Kathie Luttrell

Play dumb like a fox

In buying or selling it is not always smart to be too decisive or knowledgeable. This is one of the classic strategies - it is well used by seasoned sales people.

Sometimes saying you don't know the answer or asking the customer what they think is far better than trying to wing it. Nobody has all the answers no matter how long they have been selling.

If the customer says "your price is high" simply say "I wonder why?   Do you think the competitor is adding something in or taking something out that is making the price difference?" Ask to see the label or the invoice so you can go back to your company and find the answers.

In other words - playing dumb can be smart.

This strategy is used to draw them out with the aim of extracting more information from them. You are up against a smooth customer when this is used against you.

You will get better answers if you are slow to understand. The trouble is that most of us want to look good. We find it hard to say, "I don't know" or "tell me that again."

An excellent example of asking for help: While I was sitting in a sales managers office getting ready to go to lunch with him, his secretary announced that his 11:45 life insurance appointment was here. I volunteered to leave, but he said it would only take a few minutes and to stay put.

The young insurance man entered the office, handed the sales manager an application and said, "You don't want to buy any life insurance, do you?" That is considered the poorest choice of words a sales person could ever use.

The sales manager couldn't believe what he was hearing. He sat the insurance man down and for 15 minutes lectured him on how to sell. He told him how to use features and benefits, family protection, cash build up and education funds.

The sales manager said he was going to buy $250,000 additional coverage and began showing the young insurance man how to fill out the application. The sales manager handed the insurance salesman the completed application along with a deposit check and said, "Son, I hope you have learned never to use that opening question again?"

As the insurance man was leaving, his signed application and deposit check in hand, he turned to the sales manager and said, "Oh, I never use that line, unless I'm calling on a sales manager."

Customer surveys are basically useless because people only tell you what you want to hear. Here is a magic question that will reveal the true feelings of your customer: How can I make it better?

Q: How has our service been?
A: It has been fine.
Q: How can we make it better?

By using this additional question you are able to extract the real information you need. With this information you may be able to make changes or improvements before it's too late and you lose the customer to a more creative competitor.

~~~~~~~~~~~~~~~~~~~~~

The playing dumb strategy is a strategy that is taught to women growing up. Play dumb to men so that their ego is boosted and they will feel more important and they will feel that you need them. It usually works when I use it. I agree with Teresa (below) on this one, playing dumb could make you look incompetent to a client so you must use that strategy with caution. The last thing you want is to have the client think you are not smart enough to have his business.

Kimberly Burgess

PLAY DUMB -This one should come with a warning label "USE WITH CAUTION- IF NOT USED PROPERLY SERIOUSE HARM CAN OCCURE". You know like the labels on coffee from restaurants now- "Contents hot- may cause burning if spilled".

I completely agree on the asking open ended questions part- the more you ask the better informed you are. The better informed you are the more sales you make! My philosophy is I am not selling you something; I am solving your problems. Sometimes, in order to learn what the customer's needs are (problems they are having), it's necessary to ask a few questions. The right questions can help your customer to open up to you, and give you some insight into how you can assist them. Some great questions to ask are:

1) what is the biggest obstacle you are facing right now?
2) If you could wave a magic wand, what would you fix?
3) Tell me about your past experiences using a similar service?
4) What do you hope will happen in the next 6, 12 or 24 months?
5) How will your business be changed by this?"

Teresa Cloninger

Never make the first offer

An experienced buyer will very seldom, if ever, accept your first price. An experienced seller knows this and always presents a price higher than they expect to get.

A buyer will feel like they are not doing their job if they don't get a sales person to move down a little on price. As a seller, if you don't give them a price reduction they will feel like you out-smarted them.

When someone asks you for a price on a single item that you know is price sensitive, try and get them to give you the price they are looking for.

For example: As you start looking up the price or waiting for your computer to boot up, you might respond with: "I'll be happy to give you a price on that, by the way, what price are you looking for?"

If you do get the buyer to tell you how much he or she is willing to pay, act slightly shocked as if their opening price is low!

When you are selling, always start at your highest price whenever possible. No matter what the customer may say (such as "This is a one-time only offer; take it or leave it!"), don't take it! If they really want to make the purchase, they'll move from that price.

Don't be shy when you state your original price - put on a show of confidence. Amateurs almost always hesitate when giving their first price and professionals very seldom do.

The more you ask for in the beginning, the better. You're not being greedy - you're being smart. Eventually you will meet an acceptable compromise, but usually not in the beginning.

When you ask for a higher price, you can always come down. If you begin by asking for a higher price and you know you will settle for the lower price, everyone comes out a winner. If you start low you may end up having to go ever lower.

Here's an example: I was in Ft Myers Florida taking a tour of Thomas Edison's winter home and workshop. The tour guide told a story I will never forget.

Thomas Edison had invented the "Ticker Tape" machine and was in the buyer's office in New York to sell it for use in the New York Stock Exchange. The buyer asked Edison how much he wanted for it. Edison said, "How much will you give me?" The buyer said "$25,000". Edison said, "I'll take it!"

Later they were having dinner and the buyer said to Edison, "you were mighty quick to jump on that $25,000, I would have paid all the way up to $50,000." Edison said, "I would have taken $5,000."

That was a great story – but I couldn't help but wonder. Edison must have been doing cartwheels in his mind thinking that he was getting FIVE TIMES MORE THAN WHAT HE WAS GOING TO ASK! However, what if Edison would have said, "$25,000 – is that the best you can do?" The buyer might have gone up to $40,000.

Now Edison would really have a hard time concealing his excitement! Once again, what if Edison would have said "are you sure that is the best you can do – this is the only one like it in the world – it will do this and this and this?" The buyer might have gone up to $50,000."

Here is another real live example. I was at a convention sitting next to me was a gentlemen who had recently sold his company. He told me how he started in his garage and built the business in to huge success. When he went to negotiate the sale the buyers offered him thirty million dollars - he immediately took it. One year later they sold the company for SIXTY MILLION DOLLARS.

He said if he had only hesitated and not accepted their first offer he might have added TEN MORE MILLION to the selling price!

Of course, there may be times when you know what the competition has priced a certain item and to get the business you might go in with a lower price right up front. Other times you may be dealing with a regular customer and they might consider it a pain in the neck to have to negotiate a price week after week.

Remember the bottom line of your first offer is to view it as another tool in your strategy inventory. There are times when it would be unwise to give your lowest price first with nowhere to go - and there are other times when it would be unwise to give your highest price first as you might scare off a potential new customer.

However, if they make the first offer, you usually know which way to go on your counter offer.

It is true that these strategies are practiced worldwide. When I lived in Saudi Arabia, if you did not bargain with the shop keeper, they had no respect for you and would not come down from their highest price. If you did bargain with them, you earned their respect and their friendship, and eventually the lowest price.
Kimberly Burgess

Ahhhh in Poker (I mean sales) the adage has never been truer: The one who blinks first loses. This phenomenon is not limited to one vertical (sales) – it is true globally from the school yards, and sales offices all the way to World Peace Negotiations!

First Offer: there is NO way to avoid it; one of you HAS to go first.

Here are some strategies to help you through the process.

Strategies:

1)   The Preemptive Strike – You go first and ask what price range they are looking in.

2)   The Volley- You are asked first about price- use Bob's technique – lob the question back and inquire what range they are looking at.

3)   The Double Volley- This can be a little tricky- They asked first, you lobbed it back and then they lobbed it back to you. If you don't answer this could go on a while and the end product will probably not be very productive. The best answer will be a range- State your High Number and you MID number. Don't let them have your bottom line.

4)   The Slide: Here you go 1st and list a range (once again High to Medium) and ask where in that range they fall.

Let the negotiations begin.

NOTE: No strategy will work if you have not PREPARED before hand. You need to calculate what the highest (FAIR) profit margin number would be, what your mid point is and what is the lowest you can go and STILL be profitable. It is very important to know when the price/agreement is NO LONGER BENEFICIAL to you and your company. You must be prepared to walk away when you reach this point.

Know when to hold them and know when to fold them,
Teresa Cloninger

I was working with a new salesperson. We went into an account where we knew it was going to be price sensitive. We gave them good prices on almost every item except for their number one item, chicken wings.

I knew from research before seeing this customer that he was getting a great price on this product. We were in the ball park but not where he is now. I knew he was proud of his price he was receiving. The new sales person wanted to go rock bottom on wings but I had another strategy.

I told him our pricing was fair and he would be happy with our proposal. BUT I said, ignore the wing price because I wanted to get more detailed information. After a few questions, he disclosed how much higher we were.

I then told him if were we good on the other pricing, I will need his help with our buyers to get the wing price. I made him feel proud of his wing price.

Our goal is to be competitive on all other items, and keep the same wing price that he is paying now. We could go lower but why?

Roland Degregorio

Implying too much flexibility

If everyone is always beating you up on price, maybe it is because of the way you are presenting it. Presenting your price with implied flexibility should be used as a tool, not as the normal way you present it.

For example, if someone asks for a price on 10 cases of a product you are selling, you would not want to say; "somewhere around $149" if the price was, in fact, $149. If you were presenting a price on a service you were selling and the price was $24.90 per hour you shouldn't say "somewhere around $25." By using the term "somewhere around" you have opened the door for the buyer to assume the price is flexible.

State the price firmly like you mean it. Many people don't state the price firmly and unknowingly open up the door for the buyer to start working on their price. Sometime the person presenting the price will do so giving a range rather that a firm price.

For example: "The price is between thirty five and forty dollars per case." This response signals a lack of confidence in the price quoted and encourages the customer to start working down the price, not from forty dollars, but from thirty five dollars.

Practice delivering your price with a tone of confidence. Deliver it with the same conviction that you would use to give someone your phone number.

"What are the last four digits of your phone number?"

5197 - Not "between 5196 and 5200".

What month were you born?

October - Not "somewhere between September and November".

If you signal with words such as "about" or "roughly,'" the buyer will take this to mean that you can go lower. If you do imply flexibility follow the other rule of selling - ask for more than you expect to get, because you may need the room.

Flexibility is a tool you can use - sometimes you might want to imply a certain degree of flexibility.

For example. Lets say a customer is looking for 100 cases of your product. You know that the customer has shopped around for a couple of other quotes. Giving your price too firmly may cause you to lose the business. However, giving your highest price and slightly implying that you are willing to work with the customer will open the door to a possible sale that would otherwise be lost.

But remember - flexibility is a tool - a strategy to use when the situation calls for it.

~~~~~~~~~~~~~~~~~~~~~~~~~~~~~~~~~~~~~

I don't believe that flexibility is weakness. When you're shaking about the price and you have little to no confidence in you or your product, then that is weakness. I do think that it's important to be firm in the price and know that the price you're giving them may be a little high but the service that YOU offer is more than well worth it. If you do decide to open it and sound flexible, be firm with it. Display the confidence that if you are willing to go down, it's because you want to help that customer and you're willing to work with them not because they control the situation.
Matthew Thacker

This articles points out something that I am instilling in people that are training. People are most sold by your conviction rather than your persuasion. People have to buy YOU before they buy from you. I think with practice and role play you can cumulate the confidence you need to quote rates with authority. It's the ease that comes from practicing or real life applicable experience.
Kristan Wilson

Look them in the eye as you give them the price. It is your product, be proud of it. Think of it as "spiking" the ball after a touchdown. You know this is the best product for your customer at a fair price. Be proud of it.

Do you think people who buy a Lexus are not looked in the eye when given a price? They know they are buying the best, a product with a track record. If they wanted cheep they would have gone to the "cheapo depo" and bought a older car, at a cheaper price with less or unknown dependability.

Trip English

You say flexible, translation weakness.   Again, my hand goes in the air. I do have a problem with this, because one senior salesperson says give the best price the first time, and another says start high and come down. And which is best, it depends on the client. Sometimes high price scares away potential business, but on the other hand if you give the best price first, there is no room for negotiation… again reading your client and getting as much information from them before providing any numbers is the only way to go.

Kathie Luttrell

There is no flexibility in menu prices at a restaurant so there should be no flexibility in proposing the cost.
A roast beef sandwich is not "about 7.99".

Roland Degregorio

Making the add-on sale

Beware of the person who agrees to your price too quickly, they may plan on asking for more.

If the buyer agrees to your price too quickly there is usually a request that will be close behind.

"That price sounds pretty good, I will take 100 cases."

"By the way can I have special terms on that?"

Another customer might agree to the price right away and ask for same day or next day delivery. From a buyers perspective this is called the "add on."

Agree to the initial price and then as soon as the sales person starts ringing up their commission, drop the "add on" question. This is an also an excellent strategy for you to use as a sales person.

Once you have what you want in hand, there is a natural tendency to leave as fast as you can. Perhaps there is an unconscious fear that the customer will change their mind or cancel the order - just the opposite is true.

Once a person makes a decision, their mind works to reinforce the decision. By getting a small commitment first the buyer will start to justify the decision and it becomes easier, not harder, to add on additional items.

Why? Think about your own decision making process. Once you make a decision your mind does a search, similar to a computer doing a search for additional information. Your mind is looking for ways to justify the decision you just made.

For example. Lets say you have made the decision to buy a new house. The mortgage payment will be much higher - but you justify it by saying that the new house will have three bedrooms for the kids, a two car garage so you can park both cars inside, a better school district, a dining room so we can have the family over for holiday meals, etc.

Then you get the news that the mortgage didn't go through.

You now justify the fact that you will really be better off without the higher mortgage, the kids are fine sharing a bedroom, the two car garage isn't really necessary, the school district is not that bad and I didn't really want to have the in-laws over for holiday meals anyway.

There is always supporting information for whatever decision you make. Notice the next time you have to convince your husband, wife or family member that you made the right decision about an important family issue. Your mind will make a mental checklist of the pro's and con's. If you are "pro" watch how your mind will weigh the list in your favor - especially if you have already made a decision and a financial commitment.

Your customer's mind works the same way. This tactic is being used on you every time you buy a car. First the car sales person will get you to agree on color, then options, then an extended warranty, and before you know it you bought the car - one small piece at a time.

The last-minute add on involves throwing in an extra request (usually not so huge as to break the sale but big enough to hurt) at the final moment, just when you, the sales person, has put down your defenses and assumes you have a deal.

The add-on seems to go against a person's nature. "I got what I wanted, I better leave before he or she changes their mind."

To successfully use this tactic, stick around a while. If you are selling multiple items, sell the first one. Wait a few minutes, sell the second one. Wait a few more minutes, sell the third one, and so on. Give the buyers mind a chance to justify their decision.

Remember, they are thinking, "I bought the first one - I might as well buy the second one. I bought the second one - I might as well buy the third one."

That is how little orders turn into big orders. It is like going into the grocery store and buying a chicken.

I bought the chicken - I better buy the potatoes - the salad - the rolls - the desert - and before you know it your shopping cart is full.

~~~~~~~~~~~~~~~~~~~~~~~~~~~~~~~~~~~~~~~

"It's a good strategy to have - but not advisable to do it all the time on the same customer or they will start to think that you are milking them. Be sure to only sell the customers what they want and/or need to grow their business. Sure, rolls are nice to have with a chicken dinner, but is it really necessary or critical to have? Over negotiating, or over selling your customer may also result in them looking for a new sales rep. This is once again a very delicate balancing act."
JoAnne Welch"

I was taught to get the order signed and leave as quickly as possible. Some sales people will want to hang around and socialize for a while but this can give "buyer's remorse" time to kick in. If it happens when you are sitting in front of the customer it is very easy for him to retract or reduce his order. If you are not there he may feel that it is too late and start justifying his wise decision. However, I may have been leaving business on the table by not adding something on immediately after he decided to buy.

Crocker Smith

I make my "add ons" during stages of my presentation. for example, "You will receive this service for $X dollars, Plus "add on, add on" at no additional cost." As we discuss more ideas and options I customize the "add ons" I fell would benefit that particular customer. The customer feels you are throwing something extra in!

Being on the other side of add on sales- Say you are about to close the deal when the customer throws in the extra request that cuts your commission half!! You must be able to justify with other benefits they are receiving as "no cost add ons" already. As sales people we are in it to make money, we just have to determine what we can take for the sale.

Brooke Knight

Get something in return

Do not keep lowering your price without asking for something in return or you will make it too easy for the buyer to keep asking.

The trade off is a very basic yet important strategy when dealing with buyers. Every time you give in to one of the requests such as price reduction, marketing money, extra services, etc., the trade off strategy should go through your mind: "If I do that for the customer, what can I ask the customer to do for me?"

This is our attitude, not our actual statement. Negotiating as a seller is not the same as negotiating as a buyer. If you are selling and you get tough and walk away, at the end of the day you have not sold anything. Most of the negotiating strategies are designed for buyers and must be adjusted if used by a person trying to make a sale.

Many people complain that customers or buyers today have no loyalty. "Show a customer how to save money on a certain item and they will shop around to see if it can be purchased for a few cents cheaper from a competitor."

If customers are not loyal, perhaps it is because when you give everything you have, you do not ask for anything in return. Trading builds a relationship.

Giving and taking are part of selling; they are part of the process and not a sign of weakness! Here are a few points to keep in mind:

1. Do not assume the customer knows what you want. Make your request loud and clear!   Do not be shy about asking for something in return when a customer asks you for a price discount. If it is done in a spirit of cooperation they will not take offence.

2. Whenever you give a price reduction, be sure to ask for something in return. You are not doing anybody favors by giving away something for nothing - the customer will not respect you and you hurt your self respect.

3. Make this an important principle in your selling. Never give up anything without getting something in return (even if what you get seems trivial). The customer offers to buy the floor model of the coffee machine at a reduced price. You, instead of lowering the price, offer a 90-day free service guarantee.

4. The customer requests a lower price on a larger than normal order. You offer some additional marketing support instead.

5. The customer complains that the price is too high. You offer to sell your higher quality product line at a slightly lower price. Explain to the customer that the higher quality is an investment in their customer satisfaction.

6. Whenever lowering the price, never go down in equal increments. If you have an extra five dollars built in, go down two dollars, and if you must go down a second time, reluctantly go down another dollar and twenty five cents, a third time go down a dollar and ten cents. Each time you go down on your price ask for an additional item or something else in return.

"It's always a great idea to ask for something in return. My prospect, "if you give me the next shot at your business, I will reduce my price, but once you have benchmarked my service against your current service, we will then renegotiate my rates, does that sound fair?" Or you can use the scenario of a shortened liquidation period on the first order and then renegotiating those terms once you have your foot in the door. I once used this tactic to get business with UPS. We had 400 offices nation wide receiving our payroll checks and sending out payroll 2 times a week. I said, "if you give us the customer service business, we will switch our service from FedEx to UPS nationwide". It worked and my former company still uses UPS and they still staff UPSs Customer Service Departments."
Kristan Wilson

"In selling, the seller really does have the upper hand when it comes to negotiating the deal. The buyer will always try to low ball to see how much savings that they can get out of the deal. My sister currently has her house up for sale, and was offered a price that was $15,000 below the listed price. I advised her to go back with the original price of the house ... but should the buyer want the house at the price that they had stated, it's going to come without the fridge, stove, washer, dryer ... etc. even down to the furnace!. All I can say is her real estate agent was shocked at her reply."
JoAnne Welch

"What do you suggest that we offer that is not already included in our sales pitch? We offer to handle payroll, worker's comp, counseling, customer service, drug screens, and criminal backgrounds – which is what every agency in this area also handles. What I am looking for is something that makes Ambassador stand up and above the rest – why should they choose my services over another company?"
Angela Brewer

The one thing the competition does not have is YOU... "and one more thing, Mrs. Prospect, I go with the program - and if you don't think I can make a difference, just give me a try".
Bob Oros

"I agree, we come with the package. Not only are our clients buying our service but they get us. I tell them call me anytime if you have questions, problems, etc. I think them knowing we are available more than just regular 8-5 and are willing to go the extra mile, makes our office better than other temp services."
Sherry Tyner

"The first thing I think of in terms of trade-offs (with Ambassador) is our rate. If we lower our rate, we want to able to have more employees at that work site. If they only want one employee, we aren't going to be as willing to lower the rate. However, if they want 25 people, we can lower it substantially. Good advice, Bob."
Suzanne Davis

"You are right, often we forget and don't realize that we also have the power to negotiate. We get so locked into selling that we forget that we to can ask for something in return. Thanks for the reminder and it is my goal to try this with my next order."
Kathy Hart

"This is a great lesson I have seen this work. We have often gone down on price for larger quantities of orders. Such as 30 temps at a specified rate but should the number of employees decrease the rate will increase soon."
Crystal Brown

"This article reminds me of what the true art of selling is. Years ago people referred to buying a product from a company as "trading" with that company. Trading used to be the staple that built the relationship between the buyer and the seller. Today we are to eager to just buy or sell, and move on. There is very little trading that happens. If we begin to "trade" with our customers again, then we will build stronger, more loyal, clients."
Scott Green

"We had a customer that we got the contract even though our price was higher than the competitors. We provide employee staffing. We won the customers loyalty because we offered them more. We had a rate for the regular employees that we found for them, but if they had a person that they new and wanted to hire then we had a lower rate for them. Any time they needed more employees they new they could count on use to provide them with what they needed. We asked for them to call use for what ever their needs were and in return we gave them price adjustments."
Laura Rice

"I have used this recently in a sales call. She asked us for help in finding a particular type of person and asked if we were going to give her them. I said that it depended on what was in it for our company. Could we expect some orders from them? Also done this as a buyer in my husband's favorite store…Best Buy and it worked."
Linda Cassell

"For the most part, we do explain how we do not send just anyone for their positions. WE take the time to look for the correct person with the correct qualifications. I have done some trading when it came to direct hires, and it was in our benefit."
Pam High

"A lot of times agreeing to lower a bill rate will be agreed on if it means that we can get more temps out to this client which helps to balance out the agreement."
Marie Royal

"I believe I understand this concept well. The things I offer back or "trade off" with the customer are actually selling points to my service. For example, I offer ME, I offer insurance benefits when discussing payroll services, I offer delivery services when discussing temps, I offer personalized service and pick up and delivery of timesheets and checks all the time. There are many more options and trade off's we can offer. I learn a new one at least weekly. I also pay very close attention to my "higher authority" when she is with me and wheeling and dealing with the customer to learn what she offers."
Patsy "CiCi" Clements

"Should you ask for something in return for a price reduction? YES- Never give something for nothing. When a customer ask for a lower price ask for something in return no matter how small it might be. Or using product as a example give them a higher quality product at a reduced price and sale it as a quality to there customers."

Christal Cornacchia

"You should always ask for something in return if you are reducing your price. You are not doing anybody favors by giving away something for nothing – the customer will not respect you and you hurt your self respect. Giving and taking are part of the process and not a sign of weakness."

Stacy McDaris

The bait and switch

Retail stores often advertise fabulous but fake bargains just to get you to come in so they can sell you something more expensive. This scheme is commonly referred to as "bait and switch."

It is simple enough: they advertise some item at a price low enough to lure you into the store. But here is the switch: the advertised item is not for sale. The salespeople may give you any number of reasons why you cannot or should not buy it.

"There are not any left. . ."
"Many customers who bought it are dissatisfied . . ."
"The product just is not any good . . ."
"You cannot get delivery for six months . . ."

The truth is that these salespeople never had any intention of selling the advertised special. They kill your desire to buy it and instead try to get you to buy the item they had in mind from the beginning.

"Bait and switch" is an unfair practice and is against the law. Although you cannot always spot bait ads in advance or know that the switch is going to follow, there are a few steps you can take to avoid the trap.

First, realize that a good salesperson may try to persuade you to buy a better quality item or a different brand with more features at a higher price. There is nothing illegal or unethical about this. The important thing is that you are given a choice without undue pressure.

Keep in mind, though, that if a product or service is advertised at a price that seems too good to be true, this may be a bait ad. Then, if the merchant refuses to show you the advertised item, to take orders for it or deliver it within a reasonable time, disparages it, or demonstrates a defective sample of it, take this as a sign that you are probably being "switched."

For example: You go into a store to buy a computer you saw advertised. It was out of stock, but when a salesperson tells you a faster model is available for an additional $100, you purchased it because it was available immediately.

The deliberate use of stock outages of a featured, low-price bait brand in hope of persuading customers to switch to a more profitable substitute brand is a form of bait and switch.

If you want to see the bait and switch used, visit any car dealer. After you find the car you want you may be surprised to find your low offer immediately accepted. After getting you to commit yourself to a price the salesman will say something like, "Well this looks good." All I have to do is run this by my sales manager for approval and the car is yours:"

As you are sitting there congratulating yourself on getting such a good deal, the sales manager comes in to review the price with you. He says, "You know, Joe was a little out of line here. This price is almost $400 under our factory invoice cost." He produces an official-looking factory invoice. "You cannot possibly ask us to take a loss on the sale?"

Now you feel a little embarrassed. You are not quite sure how to respond. You thought you had a deal and Joe's bait and switch tactic just shot it down. If you stick to your guns and talk the sales manager into meeting your price, he will eventually cave in and tell you that since he is selling it under factory invoice he will have to get his manager's approval.

This game will continue as long as you can hold out against a battalion of managers.

Understand that it is a matter of perspective. While you may view this process as underhanded and deceptive, it is a time-honored negotiating tactic used everywhere in the world, from the Middle East bazaars to Mexican street markets.

My personal opinion is that although bait and switch is a long standing sales strategy. It is still under handed in my view. I would never use this tactic to sell a product. I feel that if this is used in your sales strategy then you may not have a product you believe in and shouldn't be selling it to begin with. Bait and switch can do nothing in the long run but damage your Company's and your reputation as a leader in your field.

Brian Spraggins

Another problem with the bait and switch is that they trick you into thinking that they are looking out for your best interests, saving you from purchasing the lesser item. I heard on the radio the other day a local car dealer offering SUV's for 12,000 dollars, and then at the very end they said they only had two on the lot for that price. At least they admit to the bait and switch before you get there!

Morgan Frazier

I agree that most sales people do use the bait and switch. The most common place I have seen this is in the retail industry and it really depends on if you are buying for the price, or for the need. If you need the item you may opt to buy the higher priced item that is substituted. If you are buying a luxury item you may be a little more cautious. Shopping around before making any substantial purchase can usually help avoid a bait and switch.

Kathie Luttrell

I have always heard that car salespeople use this on a daily basis. This tactic was used on me at a dealership about eight years ago but in the legal way. The type of car I wanted was advertised at a price to entice any buyer to the dealership. Of course, this was the base model. Once all of the options were added, my monthly payment would have been $80 more per month. I contemplated for 2 days. The salesperson finally said, "Why don't you come and get your car". What are you going to do? I caved but I got the car I wanted.

Gregg Nixon

Bait and switch is not a tactic I would advise using in staffing, to be quite honest. The relationships we build with our clients are generally long lasting so it would do us little good to try and use a bait and switch tactic for a short term sale if we are trying to gain the long term business. Customers would not appreciate being duped.

In fact here in Beaufort it has done us good NOT to use that type of tactic. One of our competitors tried to lowball us by approaching our biggest customer and saying that they were less expensive. Our customer took the bait, and then when they received the invoice they discovered that while the markup was indeed lower than ours, there were several added fees that were not included in the markup (they were not informed of said fees) and it ended up costing more than us in the long run. Needless to say, they don't use that agency anymore and have been loyal to us for years. In fact they had enough trust to impart that story to us!!

Marquesa Ortega

I love it when a competitor uses a bait and switch on one of my customers. I inform them that they have fallen pray to a tactic used by some sales people and I apologize for my professions sleazy side. I then inform them that what the competitor did was give them an inferior product at a reduced cost. I show them that we also have cheaper products but that they have always purchased high quality products and I did not for see them wanting to lower their quality.

Patrick

I've worked for companies that thrived on the bait and switch. The jewelry industry does this on a daily basis and usually calls the bait a "loss leader". They will lose money on the advertised item(in hopes that you can switch)just to get you in the store. A skilled salesperson can make the switch; others sell many of the loss leaders. According to which side you're on, it can be a good tactic.

Rick Hughes

My daughter and I went to a clothing store recently. This article reminds me of what we encountered. This store had big red signed hanging all over the store that said "BUY ONE GET ONE FREE ON ALL CLERANCE". So my daughter and I said great, we could by get more for our money. So we picked out several items that we liked and went to check out. When the cashier started ringing up our items they were not ringing up "BUY ON GET ONE FREE". We asked the cashier what was going on and she said that the items we picked out were not included in the buy one get one free. We asked why and the excuse was that because they were considered blue jean material they did not count in the sale. So we argued that the sighs all over the store did not say that jeans were excluded. She then called someone else, and then the manager. We did not get the answers we were looking for so we told the manager that they could keep their merchandise and we would go to another store that did not have misleading sales signs everywhere. This was defiantly a "BAIT AND SWITCH".

Laura Rice

Never split the difference

As soon as someone suggests splitting the difference, the whole game changes.

The side that makes the offer has essentially revealed what they will settle for. You, a seller, should always let the buyer be the one to offer to split the difference first.

Suppose that after the initial negotiating, you a sales person, have a price of $50 per case on a one thousand case order and the customer wants to pay $45. The buyer says, "Let's split the difference." What they have just done is raised their offer to $47.50.

The negotiating range has changed.   Before, the difference was $5. Now the difference is $2.50 per case.

What's your move? Acknowledge the offer with appropriate respect but make it clear that you cannot yet accept because the price is still too low. (Continue to maintain that the top of your limit is $50).

After waiting a few seconds, it becomes your turn to make a counter offer. But now the negotiating range is between $47.50 and $50.00. You say, "Let's meet half-way; I'll come down $1.25 and you come up $1.25."

The deal is struck at $48.75 per case. If you had been the one to offer to split the difference just the opposite might have happened. If you agree to split the difference you would have lowered your price to $47.50.

The buyer would have said to YOU: "Let's meet half-way; I'll come up $1.25 and you come down $1.25. The deal would have been struck at $46.25.

On a one thousand case order the difference would have been $2,500. (Which, of course, would have come out of your gross profit).

The first person who places a value on a product or service establishes its worth.

A perceived value must be established when the customer or buyer makes a low offer and gives you a low price. You should counter by presenting an equally high price. This is sometimes referred to as "bracketing."

~~~~~~~~~~~~~~~~~~~~~~~~~~~~~~~~~

This all revolves around confidence in your selling abilities. I am, many times, tempted to take an offer of this type or to be the first to make the 'split the difference' offer to get the sale over with. This keeps the competitor from having another shot at the deal. However, as you stated, it can cost you profit. If you are always low bid you will eventually go out of business.

Crocker Smith

When you split the difference you are in most cases going to lose money. I can't afford that, can you? Place the value on your service, establishing its worth and benefit. We too are in business to make money; we can't lose profit to gain a customer every time. If we did we would not be in business....

Brooke Knight

How customers decide

Have you ever laughed at a joke that wasn't very funny, but everybody else laughed so you felt the obligation to laugh? Have you ever bought something based on the fact that it was the "best selling" or "fastest moving" item? Would the statement "4 out of 5 people surveyed recommend this product" influence your decision? How about "over two million copies sold" on the cover of a book? Would that make you feel more comfortable about your decision to buy it? If so, you are not alone. People are highly influenced and persuaded by what others do.

I am the first customer to go through the car wash, yet the tip jar has 10 one-dollar bills folded in the jar. I am the first one in the bar and notice the bartenders tip jar already has several dollar bills in it..

Can you remember the screaming, almost hysterical fans in the front row when the Beatles performed – and Elvis – and Frank Sanatra – you guessed it – all paid to be there. Nightclub owners create long lines to give the impression that business is great. Krispy Crème Donuts has a bunch of folks camp out the night before the store opening so they can have the first donuts that are cooked – creating the impression that these donuts must be really good.

What does all this mean? It means that this concept works and it can work for you too. Here's how.

Everybody likes to think of himself or herself as a nonconformist – someone who does their own thing. You and I like to see ourselves as independent – until it comes time to make a decision – then we find out what everybody else is doing and what everybody else thinks – and conclude that they must be right – and make the decision that I am going to do the same thing.

Let's say you are a new sales person calling on a potential account. Would you say; 'I am new and don't have any customers yet – will you take a chance and be the first?"

If you were a seasoned sales person would you go into a potential customer and say; "We have great quality and excellent service?" No, you wouldn't want to say something like that because their response would be "so what." You would want to take the approach that the bartender, car wash, church, evangelical preacher and concert promoter took. You want to bring on your success stories, testimonials, references, people your prospect knows and a list of happy customers who are buying from you. You would want to put a little money in your tip jar to show that others are buying and they are happy. Why? To make them feel safe about their decision to buy from you.

One word of caution about this strategy...

When I first started using this technique of letting a customer know that several people use this product and are very happy, I had a customer reject the item that I was recommending because I told them about a competitor who was using the product. I have now modified my success stories so that the customer only hears about customers that are either not in direct competition or are geographically separated."

~~~~~~~~~~~~~~~~~~~~~~~~~~~~~~~~~~~

I made several calls on a local doctor and explained and promoted our payroll service to him. He was very skeptical at first but after the fourth call he was on board and excited about it – he could see the advantages for his practice and his employees.

He said to come by the following Monday and we would take care of all of the documents but on that Monday morning his office manager called and said that they had discussed it further and decided against it at this time. She had a defensive attitude and did not want to listen to anything I had to say.

At this point I was very tempted to "raise the level" of my tone to her but I bit my tongue and resisted. I just said '"please feel free to call me if I can help at any time". Yesterday the doctor called me and said he was ready to do the deal. His accountant had told him that this was a good thing for him to do and it would save him money (the exact same thing I had been telling him). Sometimes it takes a third party to convince a customer. I signed him up two hours later and I was able to feel comfortable around the office manager also.

But I came very close to "burning the bridge". It turns out that the office manager was also his daughter.
Crocker Smith

I've never been one to follow crowds, never bought the most popular car model, etc.   It seems to be a great marketing strategy though because a lot of people follow the crowds. I remember a guy telling me one time that McDonald's had the best hamburgers. "They had to be the best because they sold the most." I replied telling him no they do great research on where to locate their restaurants and have a great marketing campaign. It's funny how some people equate the most with best.
Cary McAfee

One of my early careers was a waiter with a chain restaurant. I wanted to move on to very upscale white table cloth restaurant in the heart of downtown where the tips would be much better. I took all my 324 comment cards, good and bad, and give them to the owner with the statement: "I would like to be a part of your team, (he was a ex-pro basketball player) and here is the best references I can give you. Most of them are outstanding, A few may not seem that good, but it's a honest review of my work." Yes I got the job and it opened up a whole new world for me.
David Vize

People base a lot of their decisions on what other people are doing. It seems to make more sense to use a product/service that someone you know is using and happy with, right? Not always. My personal belief is that price is not the ultimate factor. I believe it is the ability to persuade the customer into buying "ME." Of course the successful stories, references, and the list of companies we serve are just the "icing" on the cake. Then you tell your prospect, "You get "ME" and look who else has made this decision and its working perfectly!"
Brooke Knight

I try to be the type of person that makes up my mind based on the facts not the, "I'm doing it because every one else is doing it type." Although I have been a bartender for many years and every time I walk behind the bar I take $20.00 in ones and put them in the jar. It does work. People want to follow the crowd. If they see a bunch of ones in the jar they believe that he must be a really good bartender and stand in line waiting on me instead of getting a drink right away form a bartender with only a few dollars in there jar.

Brian Spraggins

I like this strategy, although I must say that quoting a client's competition has come back to bite me as well. People do like to follow the crowds sometimes so letting a prospect know where and who your program is working with seems to build more credibility. It's funny thing to watch a crowd (and I have been guilty of this), migrating a certain way or waiting in a line just because it is drawing the masses.

Kristan Wilson

We see this all the time (tip jars full, etc.) and it tends to work in most situations. Of course, when you're doing marketing and sales, you can't really carrying around a tip jar full of ones. But you can have an arsenal of success stories, situations that best represent your services. We can all do this!

Suzanne Davis

Control over the interview

How would you like to walk into a customer's office and have a powerful tool that will give you complete control over the conversation?

You can do it. Here's how. Before you go in to see the customer carefully list five things you want to discuss. When you are in the customers office place this list where the buyer can easily see it. Without saying a word you have just taken control.

Every buyer or customer works from a list. When you place this list in front of them they will have an IRRESISTIBLE urge to work the list and check each item off. If you don't think the buyer will give you the amount of time to cover every thing you want to talk about you can solve that problem by simply using a yellow pad and a black marker.

I discovered this by accident when I was going to call on a important account and did not have the time to prepare in advance. I took out a yellow pad and made a list of five things I wanted to talk about. When I sat down in the buyers office I set the pad on the desk where the buyer could see it. I then started talking about point number one on my list.

The conversation started to get side tracked when the buyer was interrupted by a phone call. He hung up the phone, his eyes went to my list and he started talking about point number two.

His secretary entered the room and asked him to step out for a minute. When he returned his eyes again went to the list and we began discussing point number three and then four and five.

The amazing part about this is that he never became impatient with our meeting. He seemed to know that when we completed the five points I had listed on the yellow pad were all discussed we would be finished with our meeting. There were even other sales people waiting to see him and we went over my appointment time by 25 minutes.

Try it and you will be surprised at how smoothly the sales call will go.

~~~~~~`

Being a navy recruiter we used this a lot. Based on the applicants quails we would use this in the form of brochures especially when talking to the parents. The parents would start with the top one and work thru the pile until they had them all on their side of the table including the permission form they had to sign for their child to go take the physical and join the service.
Ralph Scalici

This definitely makes sense. This tool keeps the conversation on track especially for announced interruptions. I know anytime you go to a conference or workshop they use a handout or overhead projector. This here is the same principle. I know from my past management training classes they always said, "The key to any corporation or company recruiting new management was to pick an individual that follows directions." Obviously, sales management would also follow in that category. People have not a clue their being controlled because of the way it's been done tactfully without being aggressive.

Shawn Hollis

That sounds like a great idea to me. I find that the first cold call with a busy person is more influenced by the prospect not knowing how long the meeting will take than what the content is. "When will this guy stop talking and let me get back to my important work?". If I find a customer is in this mode I tend to speed up my presentation to keep their interest which is not as effective. I will definitely try this.

Crocker Smith

In a former position we were trained to complete a call/ visit work sheet prior to our visit. On the work sheet we had our VBR (valid business reason) with a primary and secondary goal. It was a great tool to move the buying process forward. Although, I don't fill out a work sheet in my current position, I always go into a client with my Valid Business Reason and my primary goal already pre determined.

Becky Akins

Before I walk into any account I would always get an idea in my head of what I was going to discuss. 90% of the time I never made it past the first topic. At least I am on the right track. Now I will try writing things down on my note pad and using it to my advantage. I can see how this would help take a lot of the pressure off of both the customer and the salesman.

Here is something I was taught in Marine Corps. They called it the 6 P's.

"Proper Planning Prevents Piss Poor Performance".

Jason Kirouac

Don't try to impress

How would you like to have everyone you meet be super impressed with you? How would you like to have your customers tell everyone they know that you are the smartest sales person they have ever dealt with?

I am going to show you how and if you try it you will be amazed at the results. You don't have to wait until your next sales call - you can try it right now.

Go and tell your spouse, partner, coworker, neighbor, or the next person you see, that you are impressed with something they are doing.

If there is nothing obvious to be impressed about look for something. Be sincere about it. Watch their reaction. They will think you are the smartest person they know. Why? Because you are smart enough to be impressed with something they are doing.

Now try it on one of your customers. Once your customer knows that he or she sincerely impresses you, they will know you are one of the smartest sales people that ever called on them.

The first law of selling to another business is to realize that there are no such things as companies, only people. You don't sell your products to some inanimate organization that makes rational decisions based on logical data. You sell to a human, emotional, somewhat irrational person who makes the decision based on issues of ego, personality and irrationality.

With this in mind you have to use the same basic principle you use to win anyone over to your way of thinking. The person you are selling to has to like you. They must believe that you know what you are talking about before they will listen to anything you have to say.

The best way to impress your customer is to let them know, in a sincere way, that you think he or she is really something. Tell them what great work they do or what an interesting business they have.

Find something you have in common. People like people who are like them. And people believe and trust people they like.

Try to discover attitudes, likes, dislikes, family backgrounds, experiences, personality virtues or quirks, careers, goals, or values that you have in common with your customers; then emphasize them.

People reason that if you're like them in some ways, you're probably like them in other ways. Therefore, they begin to transfer trust as friend to friend. And they will buy from you.

All things in moderation; the key is sincerity and having an understanding of the subject! I have 3 Words that will help you with this: Research, Research and you got it more Research. You need to know the Company, their Product (or service) and the Decision Maker you are talking with. You are NOT going to spout information to the client. Your goal is to find content to complement your client on!!!!! NOTE: a great place to find information if the company is publicly traded is in their annual reports. This will list the company's vision, notes from the CEO, history and where they are looking to take the Company. They will be impressed in two ways. The 1st is you recognized how wonderful and smart THEY are and you did your homework. Use it!

Teresa Cloninger

In my position with our company, I work with restaurant owners. I let the customer know right away I owned 3 restaurants of my own. I get 'excited' when I notice what my customers are doing "right". No one tells a restaurant owner they are doing a great job. Customers will not tell a restaurant owner that the restaurant is exceptionally clean or decorated. They come to expect perfection.

We are in the business of details. It is these details that I note and tell the customer within minutes of our meeting. I do this with every visit. I notice right away the customers focus, from exceptionally clean restaurant, great menus to signage. If I notice the outside of the restaurant neat, clean and organized, I might even point this out during our handshake.

It is noticing and noting these details that's puts the customer at ease ....to say nothing about his/her ego...

Roland DeGregorio

When you ask for advice

How would you like to have a magic formula that would turn the toughest customer into a best friend? The next time you are faced with a really tough customer, one that always gives you a hard time about everything, try this: Ask for their advice on something.

Sound too simple? Try it and watch what happens. Ask them how they would handle a certain situation. For example, ask a customer how they would sell to a certain individual that you both know.

Ask your spouse how they would handle something. Ask a friend or neighbor how to fix something. When you say to someone "I would like to ask your advice," you can almost see the person's interest level increase.

The important point to remember when asking for advice is that it must be sincere. The best way to do that is to take notes while they are responding and pay close attention to what they are saying.

Asking for advice is an excellent way to make a person feel important, however, it also has another huge benefit. The advice you get about your company, your products, or whatever you happen to be asking about, may give you an idea that could lead to some substantial new sales.

Some examples of what you can ask advise about: New products. Changes in your service. How to sell another buyer or customer. What they think of certain product features. How can you improve your service.

Try asking for a favor. We like someone more after doing something for them. If we do someone a favor we will have a positive feeling toward that person. In our attempt to get someone to think highly of US we tend to do things for them. What you want is for the customer or prospect to DO SOMETHING FOR YOU and they will actually like you more.

Customers will find a way to buy from you if they like you. They will also find a way NOT to buy from you if they don't like you.

The reason Thomas Edison sold all his inventions was simply this: Thomas Edison only invented things people would buy. To find out what people would buy he did extensive research and asked numerous experts their advise.

How many times have we come up with a seemingly brilliant idea, only to find out after investing time and money that it was all a waste of time. Perhaps the reason might be due to not seeking expert advise on the idea or project.

There is nothing a person likes more than to be VALUED. Bob, you're right on target about asking for someone's Advise. When you ask for their advice, the internal chatter in a person mind stops and they will focus their attention on you. Advice accomplishes three different things. It shows you value them as a person; you have captured their attention (not always easy to do) and you put the client into a problem solving mode. One important point here is LISTENING, take NOTES and Don't Argue!!!! The next step is to slide seamlessly into the rest of your presentation.
What do YOU think??
Teresa Cloninger

In general, people like to help others out. It's human nature. Traditional recruiting methods teach us that rather than leaving a message that says "I am looking for a Cost Accountant", rather say "You have been referred to me as an industry leader, could you help me with a project I am working on?" This usually appeals to their sense of ego (as does soliciting their advice) and also their sense of human spirit and wanting to help others out. It doesn't hurt when they feel comfortable giving you more information than you initially requested....possibly even a referral.

Kristan Wilson

"You are right on with your strategy to ask for advice. I used this strategy the other day on a new product line I carry and I was able to submit a proposal for $26,000 to a customer who had shut me down on that same topic a week before."

Lewis Hoffman

Justify rather than discount

If you do not know the reasons that justify your price, it is important to find out what those reasons are.

The business department of a major university conducted a test on 100 companies. They divided them into three groups according to how they sold.

The first group of 30 companies sold strictly on price. The sales people had as much flexibility as they felt they needed to get the business.

The second group of 40 companies was allowed to give heavily controlled price discounts.

The third group of 30 companies gave no discounts and sold at book price.

The results...

Group one sold the least amount on a per sales person basis, earned less gross profit, return on investment was the poorest in the industry. Price buyers would search for the sales people who sell on price and try to squeeze the price even lower. The sales people constantly complained that there was no loyalty among buyers.

Group two had a higher sales per person than group one, earned a higher gross profit and had a better return on investment. The sales people complained that if they had lower prices they could sell more.

Group three had the highest per person sales, the highest gross profit and the best return on investment. THE SALES PEOPLE WERE BETTER TRAINED IN SELLING STRATEGIES AND WERE ABLE JUSTIFY THEIR PRICE RATHER THAN DISCOUNT IT!

Here are some of the things a sales person might say to justify the price:

"Yes, our price is higher - but our product has longer shelf life. You will never lose any money because of spoilage. We get it in and out of our warehouse and onto your shelf faster than any other distributor."

Then show them the comparative figures on spoilage. Highlight this benefit they cannot get anywhere else.

Or you might say: "Yes, our machine costs $30 more-but other machines can cost you twice that $30 saving every few months in repairs. Here are the frequency of repair records for our machine and for our two top competitors. "Show him the figures-and then make your big point. 'A machine that hardly ever needs service and repairs is a tremendous advantage today, when service is so expensive and hard to come by. "

Here are some reasons your buyers will pay more for.

When your customer trusts and knows what to expect from you, you gain an advantage. Consistent quality, delivery, service, and constant innovation create exceptional value in a sale.

When you can demonstrate that your products are guaranteed to arrive in perfect condition, you increase your value.

When a customer perceives that your company responds instantly to their problem, the customer will do business with you again.

Your product may cost less for operator training, a lower cost to run, and reduced cost to repair than a competitive offering.

Customers will select a technically sound company over one that's obsolete or on the brink of failure.

Your customer will pay more to eliminate and avoid headaches.

~~~~~~~~~~~~~~~~~~~~~~~~~~~~~

We must be fully informed of all of our services and be prepared for any type of question they may throw at us. If they ask us a question and we get stumped, how does that make us look? We have to be informed of not only our services and what we offer, but also on our potential clients company. Do research on them before you ever walk in their door.

Kimberly Burgess

Customers resistance change

You will almost always run into resistance when you ask someone to change. Their resistance comes from their unwillingness to let go of the status quo. People do not like to change. People resist even the best ideas.

A person resists an idea for a number of reasons. The resistance starts with a negative feeling about the product or idea. He or she has not looked into it yet. The immediate resistance is general.

First of all, there is a risk. What if the change does not pay off? Then he or she loses the cost and looks foolish. Something new means change and maybe the change will be uncomfortable. It might cause problems, and who needs problems? "I tried something like this before and it did not work out well, why take the risk?"

People in general do not want to hear about you or your idea or company. Even if you get them to listen, their generalized resistance adds strength to the objection.

However, you have to sell your ideas to get ahead. Your value to the customer cannot be known unless your products and services are tried. Be prepared for this resistance.

A lot of sales people ruin their credibility because they start to sell when the presentation is only half formed. They do not do their homework. The desire to get their idea sold is there, and it generates enough enthusiasm in them to propel them prematurely into the buyer's office and go for the close.

The buyer, motivated by his/her generalized resistance to anything new, looks for what is wrong. At this point, the buyer is NOT focusing on how to make it work. So the prospect raises some tough questions that you cannot answer. Not being prepared the sale dies.

By not being prepared you have lost more than the sale. You have lost some creditability. You have hurt your image. You have set the stage with a negative first impression.

From then on the buyer expects you to be unprepared. The buyer will look harder for holes in everything you present. And he or she figures that maybe it is a waste of time to talk with you. If they hear unsupported ideas, they will not be so willing to listen anymore.

This is the reason why many people fail at presenting their ideas. They are unprepared to overcome the resistance. They cannot handle the objections.

To overcome this resistance the best approach is to gather sufficient information about the buyer as well as the products or ideas you are going to present. Depending on what you are selling it may be necessary to make two or three information gathering calls before making the first presentation.

~~~~~~~~~~~~~~~~~~~~~~~~~~~

You will do what I say, when I tell you to and LIKE it!!!! I hope this dose not sound too familiar! Why are so many companies hiring "change managers"; because it is Human nature to resist! How do you over come this? There are a couple of ways. One: slap them upside the head and tell them to just do it (not recommended by HR). Two: use research, trust and communication to gently pull the customer into the correct way of thinking. As a change manager (IE sales person) there is no magic bullet. IF you do the due diligence, ask the right questions, involve the right people (centers of influence) and COMMUNITCATE the benefits you are much more likely to close the sale (change the situation and status quo)! It is not rocket science- but it comes pretty close.

Stirred but not shaken,

Teresa Cloninger

No one likes to change, it's that simple. And it makes sense. Why leave what you're already accustomed to and what's comfortable to you to go to something you know little to nothing about. That's our jobs as sales people. We are to provide adequate information to a potential buyer to make them want to change and then make sure we help as much as possible to make it a smooth and comfortable transition.

Matthew Thacker

People stay in loveless marriages, dead end jobs and horrible living conditions, because of resistance to change. People fear the unknown and therefore are not willing to take the first steps to change their current situations. As sales people we are responsible for gently guiding our clients into a new and better situation. This usually requires negotiation, persistence and building trust from the sales person. They have to buy you before they will buy from you.

Kristan Wilson

People get scared or annoyed with changes. Oftentimes it requires them to reach out of their comfort zone and do things differently. Not all people are open to that. In fact, most people aren't. This is a big challenge for salespeople trying to convince customers to switch services or products. It is the burden of the salesperson to adequately prove the benefit of changing and be prepared to do what it takes to help the customer make the change efficiently. The better a salesperson can communicate the benefit of the change they are asking the customer to make, the more likely the customer will buy.

Marquesa Ortega

An attitude of confidence

Always assume an attitude of confidence and purpose and never apologize for making the call.

There is a psychological law that makes human beings react and respond to the attitude and action expressed by another person. There is nothing mysterious about it, except the results that come when you put this law into effect.

Everyone wants to do the appropriate thing. Everyone wants to "rise to the occasion." We have an unconscious urge to "live up to" the expectations others have of us, or to "live down" to them. If you see that your customer or prospect is busy when you first walk into their office or warehouse do not apologize for interrupting. What will go through their mind if you do? "If you see I am busy, why are you bothering me?"

If you decide beforehand that a certain customer is going to be difficult to deal with, chances are you will approach them in a hostile manner, ready to fight. When you do this, you literally set the stage for them to act on. He or she rises to the occasion. They act the part that you have set for them to act, and you come away convinced that they really are a "tough customer," without ever realizing that your own actions and attitudes helped make them one.

In dealing with your customers, you see your own attitudes reflected back to you in their behavior. When you smile, the person in front of you smiles. When you frown, the person frowns. When you shout, the person shouts back.

Not taking yourself too seriously and acknowledging your faults and mistakes actually shows your customers that you are confident. Seeing someone you admire do something clumsy or stupid will make you like them more. When you show others that you don't take yourself too seriously it makes them fee closer to you. We like confident, self assured people, however, the truly self confident person doesn't need to let the world know how great they are.

Here is a way to have your customers perceive you as confident and enthusiastic. The most effective for making a favorable first impression is the easiest thing to do: smile. Four things are accomplished when you smile - acceptance, enthusiasm, happiness and, most importantly, confidence.

You are in control! You have the power to control the customers reaction. This takes practice, but the results are amazing.

~~~~~~~~~~~~~~~~~~~~~~~~~~~~~~~~~~~~

It is important to forget what just happened at the last call, good or bad, and what you are going to do after the one you are at. Live in the moment, focusing all your attention on this one person. Bring you smile when you enter. Be a good listener. You may be the best thing that has happened to him all day.
Jim Ruth

As salespeople we are professionals and we should never let a customer take that away from us. Enthusiasm, confidence and a positive attitude should always be a part of our calls. If the day wears on you and each call begins to sound like "You really don't want to buy from me," take a break, do something else, it's not going to get better if you don't do something about it? If you are having one of those days end it at an account that respects and admires you and that says thank you. If you go home with the wrong attitude it will start your next day off quickly in the same wrong direction.
David Vize

If a customer is too busy to see you or does not want to see you apologizing for the interruption is not going to hurt anything. You will still be shut down. And, as previously mentioned, you may gain a little respect. The next time you approach them at least they know in advance that you are sensitive to their wishes and will not be pushy with them. This could make them less defensive and more agreeable to giving you a little of their time.
Crocker Smith

Showing confidence lets the buyer now that you mean business. You know what you're talking about and you know what your doing. It shows that your not there just to waste time and can earn you respect, not only from a potential client but anyone in general.

David Bradley

You have probably had days that begin with you feeling great. As the day progresses, however, your feeling of well-being starts to slip away. By day's end, you are glad it is over. If you have had this experience, you are normal. However, even on down days, you have some control. Your control begins when you decide that YOU are responsible for the attitude you display. I strongly believe that your attitude affects everyone that makes contact with you either in person or over the telephone. Your attitude is not only reflected by your tone of voice but also by the way you stand or sit, and by your facial expressions. You have the choice to reflect a positive attitude or your can go with a less desirable choice.

Yessie Narvaez

We need to have confidence before we walk through the door. If the person on the other side of the desk senses that we are not confident, even a little, they will not have much confidence in us. As far as apologizing goes, it's somewhere in between. We need to acknowledge they may be busy and we appreciate the time they are giving us, but we do not need to apologize for doing our job. As salespeople that's what we do, call on people, and at times they are busy and at other times they are not.

Brandon Sanchez

I've noticed this myself when I go to do a sales call. When I smile and at least act like I'm interested in being there, they are much more receptive and friendly. I also have a comment regarding the comment that is listed. You may feel that apologizing is a sign of showing respect but ask yourself this: Why am I going to apologize for doing my job? There are better things to say then 'I'm sorry for interrupting your busy schedule.' Instead, try "I see that your busy so I'll be brief." It gives the recognition that they are a busy person but you're not apologizing for doing your job.
Matthew Thacker

I agree with Linda that acknowledging a person is busy is a show of respect and that you value their time as much as they do. I appreciate the same courtesy when I am in the middle of something that has a deadline or is of need of immediate attention. When someone is in depth with a project I feel their mind is focused on the task at hand. The majority of what I am trying to say to them is half heard and as the old saying goes "In one ear and out the other." I do agree that attitudes are reflected by others. Reflections of actions begin as early as childhood and continue to develop through out our lives. The best example is when a child is upset and yells or raises their voice they are provoking the parent into displaying the same behavior or action but having the attitude of confidence and control will be detected and the poor behavior will circumcise.

Carla McCrea

You want to portray confidence every time you talk to a prospect or client because if you don't believe in yourself , no one else will. It's important you communicate with clients and prospects in a manner where you feel and know that your services can benefit them and that you have the knowledge and resources to fulfill their needs and answer their questions. If you come across as clueless and unsure of yourself, they will either a) not buy from you, or b) walk all over you.

Marquesa Ortega

You ever find yourself driving to work in the mornings, trying to dodge the red lights, cursing at drivers going slower than you? Are you going 80 mph answering emails, listening to voice mails, trying to type, drive and talk while behind the wheel? This all leads to your attitude that slaps your customer in the face on your first call of the day. Wake up 10 or 30 minutes earlier and get a head start. Have all your paperwork ready the night before. I devote one day to get totally organized (usually it's on the weekend when I have time) creating my weekly specials, getting show invitations ready. Not by just filling them out, but with a cover letter, a real nice presentation. I also go through all the trade magazines and make copies for my customers. Also when the brokers come by with coupons I sort them out by customer, fill them out for them with the appropriate invoices. I may not be the highest in sales, but I try to give my customers something different than the usual sales rep. Quality over quantity sometimes is best.

Trip English

I agree with everything in this section except the part about not apologizing if you see your customer is busy and you are interrupting them. To me it is a sign of respect and a sign that you are aware of the situation they are in and not ignoring it. I believe that one could still show confidence and acknowledge someone's busy schedule.

Linda Cassell

www.ingramcontent.com/pod-product-compliance
Lightning Source LLC
Chambersburg PA
CBHW032019170526

45157CB00002B/768